P9-CNI-661

learning to breathe

ONE WOMAN'S JOURNEY
OF SPIRIT AND SURVIVAL

learning
to
breathe

alison wright

HUDSON
STREET
PRESS

HUDSON STREET PRESS
Published by Penguin Group
Penguin Group (USA) Inc., 375 Hudson Street, New York, New York 10014, USA •
Penguin Group (Canada), 90 Eglinton Avenue East, Suite 700, Toronto, Ontario, Canada
M4P 2Y3 (a division of Pearson Penguin Canada Inc.) • Penguin Books Ltd, 80 Strand,
London WC2R 0RL, England • Penguin Ireland, 25 St Stephen's Green, Dublin 2, Ireland
(a division of Penguin Books Ltd) • Penguin Group (Australia), 250 Camberwell Road,
Camberwell, Victoria 3124, Australia (a division of Pearson Australia Group Pty Ltd) •
Penguin Books India Pvt Ltd, 11 Community Centre, Panchsheel Park, New Delhi – 110
017, India • Penguin Group (NZ), 67 Apollo Drive, Rosedale, North Shore 0632, New
Zealand (a division of Pearson New Zealand Ltd) • Penguin Books (South Africa) (Pty) Ltd,
24 Sturdee Avenue, Rosebank, Johannesburg 2196, South Africa

Penguin Books Ltd, Registered Offices: 80 Strand, London WC2R 0RL, England

First published by Hudson Street Press, a member of Penguin Group (USA) Inc.

First printing, August 2008
10   9   8   7   6   5   4   3   2   1

REGISTERED TRADEMARK—MARCA REGISTRADA
Hudson
Street
Press

LIBRARY OF CONGRESS CATALOGING-IN-PUBLICATION DATA
Wright, Alison, 1961–
    Learning to breathe : one woman's journey of spirit and survival / Alison Wright.
       p. cm.
    ISBN 978-1-59463-046-0 (alk. paper)
    1. Wright, Alison, 1961–   2. Photojournalists—United States—Biography. 3. Buddhism.
I. Title.
    TR140.W75A3 2008
    770.92—dc22
    [B]   2008022742

Printed in the United States of America
Set in Horley Old Style
Designed by Eve L. Kirch

With love, to Andrew, Claire, Hannah, and Erin

And to those who were there to help me that day—
without you I wouldn't be here to write this book

THE DALAI LAMA

FOREWORD

To make our lives meaningful takes courage. The heroes of
Tibetan Buddhism, Bodhisattvas who work to develop
compassion and wisdom, their hearts set on achieving
enlightenment for the sake of all sentient beings, have it.
Many of the Tibetans that Alison Wright has befriended inside
Tibet and in exile, struggling to maintain their identity and
heritage, have it; and she says their dedication has inspired
her. And finally, the author of this book herself, who suffered
shocking and potentially disabling injury in a road accident
has displayed remarkable courage. Alison Wright's story of
her recovery and eventual pilgrimage to Mount Kailash in
Tibet make clear that if you have courage powered by the
resolute determination to never give up, you can achieve what
others consider to be impossible.

December 20, 2007

INTRODUCTION

"One step at a time, one breath at a time" is my mantra as I struggle up the snowy 18,700-foot Dolma pass, icy wind whistling around my head and searing my lungs. My stomach churns and my head aches from altitude sickness, but my spirits are buoyed by the Tibetan pilgrims who trudge with me on this sacred thirty-three-mile circumambulation of Mount Kailash, the holiest peak in Tibet.

Despite the cold and the blinding snow, I stop at the crest of the pass to rest and have a warm drink. Pungent incense wafts through the thin air. I join my companions in adding to an array of prayer flags, which whip so hard in the wind they sound like horses' hooves drumming the ground. Each color symbolizes an element: earth, fire, water, and *lung,* or wind. We tie the flags to the lines strung up at the mountaintop, so the prayers will blow to the heavens. Kneeling, I make an altar by propping up photos of Claire, Hannah, and Erin—my three young nieces—with the colorful hand-painted rocks they gave me to leave at the pinnacle of my pilgrimage.

Both Buddhists and Hindus believe Mount Kailash to be the center of the universe. It is considered so powerful that simply visualizing loved ones here will bring them good fortune. Circling it is said to cleanse one's karma: each circumambulation inches you closer to nirvana and washes away a lifetime of sins. As I plod along, I can see pilgrims scattered along the path far ahead and far behind me, some of them creeping along one prostration at a time. It is humbling to be surrounded by such unwavering faith and devotion.

Even as my lungs labor and my legs protest, I feel a huge wave of gratitude wash over me, a prayer of thanks that I'm alive and that I've recovered the strength to make this journey. Many Tibetans save for years and travel hundreds or even thousands of miles to perform the *kora,* this ritual trek around the mountain. But for me, this is more than the fulfillment of a fifteen-year dream. Every step is a celebration of the life I nearly lost and a symbol of the physical and emotional challenges I've faced in my long, arduous healing.

I am a photographer. I have spent a lifetime immersed in other cultures, documenting the human condition in a quest to understand the world around me. Living in Asia has led me to insightful encounters with the Dalai Lama; Aung San Suu Kyi, living under house arrest in Burma (the politically correct name for the country that the military junta, her captors, have attempted to re-name Myanmar); and Thich Nhat Hanh, a Vietnamese monk and teacher who for years was exiled from his country. I admire their courage and fearlessness.

I aspired to develop their attributes of wisdom and compassion in my own heart while documenting the human dramas and devastating social conditions—the poverty, disease, and suffering—unfolding around me. I strived to find a way to balance my not-so-subtle yearning for a sense of inner peace while bearing witness to life's atrocities and injustices.

Apparently, the universe felt I needed more than a gentle nudge. In fact, it took the impact of a one-ton logging truck to find it.

learning to breathe

Life is not measured by the number of breaths we take, but by the moments that take our breath away.

—BOYD PALMER

For a long time it had seemed to me that life was about to begin . . . But there was always some obstacle in the way, something to be gotten through first, some unfinished business, time still to be served, a debt to be paid. Then life would begin. At last it dawned on me that these obstacles were my life.

—ALFRED D. SOUZA

PART I

a dance with death

When we walk to the edge of all light we have
and take that first step into the darkness of the unknown
we must believe one of two things will happen—
There will be something solid for us to stand on.
Or, we will be taught how to fly.

—PATRICK OVERTON

CHAPTER I

The air was heavy with dust and smelled thickly of burned rubber, of brakes and tires pushed beyond their limits. The midday sun was unforgiving. Birds screeched from the bamboo forest, seeming to echo the anguished cries of the injured. In the distance, I could hear muffled voices calling, "My God, someone do something! This woman is bleeding to death!"

I silently prayed that someone would help that woman, whoever she was. Time seemed to have come to such a grinding standstill that I turned my head to look at my watch. I saw deep arm-length gashes, open flesh that looked like it had been attacked by a shark, and a dark wine color rapidly spreading across the front of a light blue sleeveless denim shirt.

That's when I realized the woman they were talking about was me.

* * *

Less than an hour before, I had been sitting quietly, looking out the window of a bus. I was on a mountain road in Laos, the windiest road I had ever seen. Each turn along the narrow switchbacks took my breath away. Rising from the deep dark valleys were green undulating hills adorned with bamboo wisps and surprising bursts of yellow sunflowers; craggy limestone towers emerged from their depths. We sped along, hugging the edges.

The bus had an extra row of plastic chairs running up the middle of the aisle to accommodate all the additional passengers who were picked up along the way that day, and for many it was standing room only. I had boarded early and was lucky to get a seat, although I am fairly small, so I still had to sit with my knees jammed up against the hard seat in front of me. The passengers swayed like drunks, back and forth with each curve.

I was sleepy. I had risen at 4:00 A.M. to photograph Buddhist monks collecting alms in the northern town of Luang Prabang, but the appeal of making one more beautiful picture before heading to the southern part of Laos was worth the predawn start. I followed the string of saffron robes as the monks wound their way through the fog-shrouded streets. The local townspeople knelt in respect and filled the alms bowls with offerings of rice, sweets, and fruit. This was all the food the monks would have that day. This ancient custom was a lovely image to take away with me as I embarked on the rest of my journey.

Seeing the monks made me look forward to the three-week

retreat of silent meditation I would be attending in India right
after this Laos trip. Every year I tried to carve time to regroup out
of my rather intense, nomadic life of perpetual travel on a long
global road. I spent—and still do—more time sleeping in hotels
than in my own bed in San Francisco but somehow managed to
intertwine a career doing the photography I love with an ongoing
spiritual quest.

For years I made Southeast Asia my second home, and although
my assignments now take me all over the world, it continues to be
my favorite place to visit. I feel comfortable there. That morning
on the bus, I had recently finished leading a group on a photo tour
through Tibet, Nepal, and Bhutan. But I was now traveling on my
own, and in Laos for the first time, working on a project I loved: a
photographic book about children in developing countries.

Even though they lived in places that were often poor or suffering from the effects of war or other social ills, these children
survived with a tenacity and resiliency that never ceased to inspire
me. Their openness and laughter touched me to the core; there
was such simple joy in their faces as they played. Whether they
were pulling cigarette boxes on strings, flying plastic bags like
kites, or spinning tire hoops with a stick, they emanated a purity
and contentment all too often missing in the youth of "more developed" countries. Their courage and optimism was impressive,
their enthusiasm delightful. They were such a reflection of the
societies in which they lived. My purpose was a simple one: to
celebrate their spirit and their heritage. I didn't have kids myself,

but after every trip it seemed as if I'd come home with a backpack full of them.

In Laos I had been traveling through remote northern regions, photographing hill tribes. Laos is a patchwork of sixty-eight different ethnic groups, a landlocked communist country of only six million people, which has only recently opened its doors to tourism, bringing a slew of backpackers eager to get high with the hill tribes in Muang Sing. Drugs are one of the country's main means of support, and Laos is now the world's third-largest opium producer after Afghanistan and Burma. In my travels, children had approached me not only to beg a few coins but also to peddle drugs. Laos is said to have more than sixty-three thousand opium addicts.

I was there during the Hmong New Year, the time when the young people play courtship ball. In a daylong celebration, lines of girls and boys throw balls back and forth. Girls single out their favorite boy and let him know they like him by throwing the ball mainly to him. Clothing is their banking system, and the Hmong girls were dressed in their elaborate best, purchased with money sent by relatives in the United States.

During the Vietnam War, the American government was reluctant to send many of its own troops into Laos and encouraged the Laotian people to fight the communist Vietnamese on their own land. Because of their Buddhist beliefs, many Laotians refused to take up the guns that were given to them. The CIA therefore recruited these tough Hmong tribesmen to fight the Pathet Lao and North Vietnamese. More than thirty thousand—a tenth of the tribe—were killed.

From 1964 to 1973, U.S. warplanes dropped about two million tons of bombs in the jungles of eastern Laos—an average of one planeload of bombs every eight minutes, around the clock, for nine years. Up to 30 percent of them didn't explode. This has deeply affected the Laotian economy by rendering much of the land useless. These potentially lethal cluster bomblets, or *bombis*, continue to endanger the Laotian people, mostly field workers and children who mistake them for colorful toys. It was issues like these that I hoped to bring to light in my book.

Because of these ubiquitous land mines and recent attacks by guerrilla insurgents, I traveled mostly by river and tried to avoid the roads. On my thirty-eighth birthday, two days before Christmas, I had disembarked from a riverboat and wandered around Nong Khiaw, a small village situated on the Mekong River. I was feeling one of those twinges of loneliness that sometimes accompanies life on the road in a distant country. Just as I was wondering what my friends back home were doing, a tiny girl raced up to me and shyly handed me a pink flower. She made no indication that she wanted anything in return. Her long dark hair was matted, and as she grinned I could see that her teeth were rotted to small black stumps. She arrived with her gift at just the right moment, a reminder that the little things in life are the most precious.

Thinking of her brought a smile to my face. Bouncing along in that bus I was fulfilling my dreams: life was just what I wanted it to be. But travel is not always as glamorous as one imagines; sometimes it's simply exhausting. The mountain road continued to wind, and finally the early morning start caught up with me. Despite the uncomfortable wooden seat I was sitting on, I fell asleep.

When I awoke, the morning chill had dissipated and the midafternoon sun was warming the crowded bus. I removed my fleece jacket and pushed the window open to get some air. I didn't like the look of the glass for some reason. The young blonde woman behind me was cold and kept sliding it closed. Despite our little back-and-forth, I was insistent—little did I know that leaving it open would be one of the best moves of my life.

We were five hours into our journey as the bus lumbered along, slowing down temporarily as the driver pulled in his side mirrors and squeezed between two trucks stalled on the narrow road. Our driver seemed emboldened by the cheers of encouragement from the passengers and continued on, this time more cavalierly, picking up speed to make up for odd bits of lost time. I was glad: I wanted to get to my destination, Vang Vieng, as fast as possible. I was hoping to arrive in time to take some pictures in the late-afternoon light, but, then, I always wanted to get places faster, to cram in as much as possible. I couldn't bear the thought of wasting a moment in my life.

I'd been on the road for twelve weeks. With my guidebook on

my lap, I brought to mind the last few days, which I had spent with friends in Luang Prabang: Joe and Lynne Cummings and Jerry Alexander, whom I'd just met and who was also a photographer. They had flown in from Thailand where all three of them were based. I enjoyed meeting new people on the road, but after a quiet Christmas with the locals, drinking *lao-Lao,* the harsh local rice wine, I was looking forward to spending time with old friends.

I had known Joe Cummings for years. The lanky, soft-spoken Asia-phile knows Laos and Thailand like the back of his hand—he is, after all, the author of the Lonely Planet guides to those countries. Practically every foreigner we saw had their nose buried in his Laos book, and we jokingly made the *ka-ching* sound every time someone walked by carrying it. The group of us rented bicycles with no brakes and explored the smaller, less-visited temples. We skinny-dipped in rivers and laughed all day. It was a wonderful way to approach the New Year.

On New Year's Eve another friend, Oliver Bandmann, hosted a small party. With his flamboyant charm and chiseled features, the owner of Baan Khily Gallery in Luang Prabang welcomed us into his cozy teak home decorated with wooden Buddhas and paintings by local artists. Oliver loved a good party. Handsome young Laotian boys who worked in his home and his gallery served us a feast of local food: steamed fish rolled in *khai paen,* the local river moss; vegetable spring rolls adorned with fresh mint; fish marinated in coconut milk; and minced duck *laap*—all accompanied by a fine, crisp French wine.

"But wait, my dear friends, I have another surprise for you," Oliver said, clapping his hands in excitement and shooing us out of his house and down to the nearby Mekong River. A cascade of candles illuminated the steps leading down to the water's edge, where we found a cluster of lanterns Oliver had made from the local *saa,* or mulberry, paper.

The lighting of the lanterns, or *khom loy,* symbolizes the spirits rising to the heavens, and it is believed that all misfortune will float away with them. We wrote our New Year's wishes onto the lanterns' paper tails, scrawling messages of peace, freedom, harmony, and safety from harm for our friends and family. My note was a simple, one-word plea: "Love." Once lit, their heat lifted the lanterns high into the air. In deference to the new millennium, we released twenty in all, one in honor of each century. I was amazed that they could fly so high; their pinpoints of light seemed to mingle with the stars.

Suddenly, the serene scene was shattered by the sound of gunshots, and we turned to see a truckload of drunken Laotian soldiers clamoring down the steps toward us. We sobered up instantly. When the soldiers reached us, one of them poked my ribs with his rifle and ordered me toward the waiting vehicle. At first I was afraid, and then I was angry.

"What are you, crazy? Get that fucking thing out of my back," I shouted, pushing the muzzle tip away from my body. In the confusion, we watched as Oliver and his coworkers were hauled off and loaded into the back of the truck. The soldiers called out in peals of insane laughter, shooting their rifles into the air. Jerry, Lynne, Joe, and a small group of us were left in a blanket of heavy exhaust fumes, watching, stunned, as our friends were driven off into the blackness.

We waited back at Oliver's place in a somber mood, drinking the rest of the champagne and cleaning up the dinner dishes. I looked at the clock; it was just after midnight. "I certainly hope this isn't an omen for the upcoming year," I said.

The next day, our friends returned—after a night of verbal abuse, securing their freedom was simply a matter of money. The soldiers had initially claimed that we were sending illicit messages to guerrillas. Since he could speak Laotian, Joe had gone to help negotiate their freedom.

I had planned to leave for Vang Vieng on New Year's Day, but this little drama put me a day behind schedule. After photographing the monks, I joined Jerry for breakfast at a small coffee shop on the main street. We exchanged business cards, which is how we learned each other's last name. As I swigged down the last of my coffee, I realized that by stopping to eat I had missed the bus I had planned to take. With a quick hug, I raced off to the bus depot, and I was pleased to find the next bus to Vang Vieng already parked and waiting in the station. For some reason I felt uneasy as soon as I boarded. I changed my place three times, and then settled on a seat on the driver's side near the front. Stowing my bags underneath the rickety wooden seats, I calmed down. I'd ridden buses in worse shape than this one all over the world.

Lost in my memories of the New Year's Eve party and the soldiers' drunken abuse, I had just shifted my gaze from the scenery when I saw a massive blue truck rounding the corner toward us. We were taking the hairpin turn too fast, and both vehicles had crept into the center divide. The truck was a jerry-rigged rural bus, an open logging trailer crammed full of people. As it barreled toward us, I had a fleeting glimpse of the passengers' shocked faces, and in a flash I remember thinking, "What a near miss!"

CHAPTER 2

I sat directly at the point of impact.

Glass shattered, metal exploded, people shrieked. The blue truck's cab had cleared the front corner of our bus, but as we took the curve it crashed into our side. My hand instinctively flew up to protect my face. My head bashed against the hard steel frame of the window; then I felt my whole left side twist and snap. There was a momentary feeling of surprise as all the air slammed out of my body, and then I was blinded by a bright white light. I had to pause and ask myself if I had died.

No, still conscious. Ever the photographer, my next thought was to grab my film, but I couldn't lift my body. The blue nose of the logging truck had split through the side of the bus and pinned my legs between two seats, which had crumpled into each other. The force of the impact had left a streak of baby blue paint

13

running down my black pants. Quickly, the inside of the bus was filling with dense smoke.

"Get off the bus! The bus is on fire!" a woman screamed as a stream of people filed passed me.

"Don't panic, just walk off," said a calm voice behind her.

People were shouting and pushing their way down the aisle in hysterics, but I couldn't move. As smoke billowed around me, I knew I had to get myself off the bus or I was going to burn inside it. With no help on the way, it would be up to me.

I decided to forget my camera bag. In some kind of adrenaline rush, I managed to push apart the mangled metal of the seats. I was free, but my legs refused to work. I was now alone. I concentrated all my hopes on the shaft of light spilling through the open front door.

I used my upper body strength to pull myself along, dragging my nonresponsive legs down the aisle, grabbing one seat after another. I lunged through the open door, fell to the ground, and simply lay on the road. Watching. Breathing in. Breathing out.

I lay utterly still and silent in the midst of circling commotion. I turned my head and that's when I realized my left arm was perforated with shards of broken glass. The bus looked as though it had split open like an overripe watermelon, its bloodied human contents spilling out from all sides. A blonde woman with a head gash was dangling between the two vehicles. Beneath her, a young dreadlocked backpacker, his gaze fixed at the sky, leaned against the wheel hub, with a long metal rod piercing his cheek. Stunned passengers stumbled about in a daze. Others cried out in terror. A Laotian girl with severe facial lacerations tripped along the road unsteadily, groping the air blindly. It was mayhem in slow motion. A body in the road lay covered in a sheet.

A woman walked by and told me I needed to get up and move out of the road.

"I can't. I can't walk," I rasped. "I think my back is broken." If I were going to die on this road I wanted some identification on me. And if I were going to live, then for sure I wanted all the film I'd just shot. So I begged her, "Can you please go back on the bus for my film and my money belt? Please?"

She kindly did so, and after some confusion over which one was mine, gently placed my black daypack beside me.

A pair of feet in sandals paused in front of my face. They were attached to a young Japanese passenger who tossed an aspirin wrapped in tinfoil down to me. It bounced off my chest. There was no way I could open it with my incapacitated arm. The thought of swallowing it made me realize that I was unbearably thirsty. "Is this the extent of my aid?" I thought. Panic began to swell against the stifling tightness in my chest. I tried to take a deep breath and, somewhat alarmed, realized that I couldn't. The anxiety rose to my throat. "Okay, someone must be doing something to get some help," I convinced myself. I was so dehydrated I didn't even cry. I didn't want to waste my tears.

A Laotian woman on the side of the road had other ideas; she was sobbing uncontrollably. Her sister was the one who had deep facial cuts from being thrown through the windshield. The locals were making a poultice from roadside plants to stop the bleeding. Another passenger was chewing wild herbs, which she placed on her open wounds.

It occurred to me that I could ask them to call the U.S. embassy until my dying breath, but they simply wouldn't understand. None of them spoke any English.

Consciously willing myself not to die, I concentrated on my breath, the life force fighting its way into my lungs. I could make shallow inhalations through my nose, but I couldn't seem to get any air into my chest. I knew that each breath might be my last. With this realization, I felt so aware, so clearheaded and completely there in the present moment.

My other anchor was pain. As long as I could feel it, I knew I was alive. I discovered that focusing on my breathing not only helped me remain alert but calmed me, slowing my heart rate and the bleeding. I never lost consciousness or went into deep shock. I'm convinced that my meditation practice is what saved my life. Being unable to move probably helped me too, because what I didn't know at the time was that my insides were a jumble, and I was bleeding to death both inside and out.

I lay on the road for over an hour, precious moments ticking by. Emergency room workers refer to this as "the golden hour." After a trauma injury the human body can more or less hold itself together and maintain blood pressure despite internal bleeding from a ruptured organ. Once an hour has passed, however, the odds of survival drop precipitously.

It would be a total of fourteen hours before I received any real medical treatment.

At the time, there was so much guerrilla warfare in the area that no one would stop their car for us. Because of its hidden curves there had been a number of violent armed attacks and robberies on this jungle road. The injured and those helping us were well aware of the danger and the fact that we were easy targets. It took over an hour for some of the uninjured passengers to flag down a passing pickup truck. The most battered of us were loaded onto its open bed. A tangle of limbs and bodies on top of one another, we bounced along for nearly another hour until we reached the small town of Kasi, where there was supposed to be medical care. I knew then that if my back was broken I would be in real trouble after this ride.

Eventually, we pulled to a blessed halt. An English-speaking fellow passenger jumped from the front of the cab and announced that we'd arrived at the clinic. Through my haze I noticed cows grazing on the grass in front of the building. Two men ran out, lifted me from the back of the truck, and laid me on the ground of a bare cement room whose walls were covered with cobwebs. I had lost so much blood that I felt faint, and I made no attempt to lift my cheek from the dirty hard floor. As I lay there with a few of the other wounded, the severity of the situation hit me anew. "This is bad," I mumbled to myself. "This is really bad."

The locals at the clinic seemed overwhelmed. After a while, a young man wearing a clean white T-shirt placed me on a table. He muttered something brusquely in Laotian to his companions but not a word to me. A woman doused my open wounds with alcohol. At least the smell kept me from passing out as the man extracted the larger pieces of protruding glass and sharp fragments of metal. Even so, in his haste he had to ignore much of the glass and gravel.

I feel light-headed at even the sight of a needle so couldn't bear to look as he began to stitch up my arm. There were no painkillers, and I had no idea if the needle he used to sew me up was even sterile. The agony was more than I would have thought it possible to endure. "We're in the Golden Triangle, for God's sake," I gasped, grabbing the collar of the female assistant who was doing her best to keep me from going through the ceiling. "Don't you have any of that opium you're all smoking up here?" No one understood what I was saying, of course. I turned back to the young man sewing up my arm. His bloodstained T-shirt was no longer white.

I willed myself to stay conscious.

I tried to think of anything, and my mind ran to my younger brother, Andrew. He was the accident-inclined one in the family. When he was four he wanted a piggyback ride and jumped on the back of a construction worker who was installing a floor in our house. As he slid down his back, a box cutter jutting from the worker's back pocket slit Andrew's stomach open like a gutted fish. Years later, while in high school, Andrew was home alone and decided to stuff matches into a metal pipe for reasons only a fourteen-year-old boy could possibly understand. When the pipe exploded, Andrew's thumb and two fingers flew across the room. Fortunately, he had the presence of mind to pick them up, put them on ice (I never could use those ice-cube trays again), and the surgeon managed to reattach his thumb and part of his fingers, with the loss of only one and a half digits. Even though I'd never broken a bone in my life, there in Laos, as the needle carved its way back and forth through the flesh of my arm, I realized that you have no idea what you are capable of until you're forced to find out.

A Western woman with a clipped accent stopped in to see me while I was being stitched up. Finally, someone who spoke some English! I was now gulping for air.

"I can't breathe. Please tell someone I need oxygen," I pleaded.

She looked at me coldly. "You can't breathe because you're afraid," she said. And with that, she turned and walked out of the room.

After my arm was sewn up, I was moved onto a straw mat across the grass lawn, past the munching cows, and laid out on a wooden bed in another whitewashed concrete room. I was changed out of my bloody black pants and into my shorts. I was cold. I was aware of movement around me; some of the other foreigners who had been on the bus were trying to figure out what they could do to help.

"We're desperately trying to find some way to get you out of here," a fair-haired Englishman said. I recognized him as the one who had come from the accident site. "About twenty others were injured in the crash, although you're in the worst shape of anyone who was brought here."

"Was anyone killed?" I whispered, thinking of the figure I'd seen under the sheet.

"We believe at least two," he told me, "including, we think, one of the drivers." A high price to pay, I thought, since both vehicles had been in the middle of the road and neither had honked its horn in warning.

A few minutes later I overheard people murmuring to each other at the foot of my bed; apparently the woman who had stopped in while my arm was being sutured was from the German embassy and had been traveling behind our bus. But she had left. She didn't want blood in her car.

At first I was so focused on surviving that my brain blocked out the pain. Endorphins (the "morphine within") had kicked in, but now my body seemed intent on letting me know how injured I actually was. My nerve endings screamed.

I thought back to the hours I had sat in meditation, fixating on the sensation of my leg falling asleep. That discomfort could hardly compare to the torment of these injuries, but it helped me to work with the pain. So much for my planned three-week meditation retreat in India. Instead, focusing on my breathing had turned out to be the practice of my life. For my life.

I floated in and out of time.

I was frustrated that no one could do more. Why couldn't anyone help? I was incredulous that I was going to die just because no one was able to get us out of there. I was told that no one had a car and that there weren't even phones in Kasi. That's when I realized that it didn't matter how much money or how many credit cards I had. I was stuck there just like everyone else.

A young Dutch couple, Roel and Meia, had been sitting behind me on the bus. I recognized her as the person who kept closing the window and also as the woman who'd been suspended between the two mangled buses. Meia had broken her arm and suffered a severe concussion. Roel, who had just proposed to Meia the day before, was desperately worried about his girlfriend but otherwise unscathed. He saw that I was alone and made sure to keep checking on me. He put a backpack under my head to make me more comfortable and took off my watch when he noticed how much my arm had begun to swell. He also told me that despite having a black eye and the fact that my hair was matted with glass and blood from my wounds, my face seemed intact. I didn't want to look for myself. If the window hadn't been open, my head would have gone right through the glass instead of just slamming into the metal frame, and I dreaded to think what might have happened.

My breathing continued to be dangerously labored. When I could no longer speak, I wrote notes. The young Englishman returned periodically, giving me hope with his updates. "We have a helicopter coming!" he assured me. But then the crushing news: "No helicopter. They won't fly at night."

Opening my eyes, I was surprised to see that darkness had fallen.

At that moment I believed I was going to die. It wasn't resignation, just an incredible clarity. Up until that point I had felt I was going to be saved. But no, this was it—my number was up. I was not going to move any farther than this wooden bed in this concrete room in this small village in Laos. I was going to die a terribly painful death. I felt just a little scared. And I was sad.

I briefly thought about all the work I was always trying to catch up on. There was a feeling of relief: it was now never going to get done and really it didn't matter. But my thoughts kept reverting back to my friends and family. I reflected on my life and the questions arose and lingered: Had I lived well, loved well? I know I had certainly packed as much as I could into my life; it sometimes felt like a suitcase I couldn't close. And now I was tired . . . so tired. I desperately wanted to close my eyes and sleep.

But I had to let my family know that I didn't die frightened and alone. I wrote a note to my brother. I told him how and where I had died. I said good-bye to Claire, his daughter, and Hannah, her newborn sister: "I just wanted to let you know that my bus crashed on a road in Laos. I'm not sure how long it's been, but it's clear that I'm not going to make it through the night. I simply can't breathe any longer. I just want you to know that I'm not afraid. Just sad that I'm never going to meet my new niece."

My last scrawled message to Roel pleaded him to "Please call my brother, Andrew. His number is in my phone book. Tell him what happened. And please give him this note from me."

As I closed my eyes and surrendered, an amazing thing happened: I let go of all fear. My body took on a lightness as it was released from its profound suffering. I felt my heart expand, free of attachment and longing. A perfect calm came over me, a bone-deep peace I could never have previously imagined. There was nothing left to do, nowhere left to go. There was also the realization that there was no need to be afraid; everything felt as though it was exactly as it was meant to be.

In that moment, I felt my spiritual beliefs transform into undeniable truths. As I lay there, I felt how interwoven every human spirit is with every other in the seamless mesh of the universe. It occurred to me that the opposite of death is not life but love. I felt myself rise and emerge from the shell of pain laying below and, as I did so, realized that leaving the body only ends life, not our interconnectedness with those whom we care about.

I thought of the written wish that only hours before I had attached to the tail of a lantern of brightness and watched sail high into the dark evening sky, absorbed by the very heavens that now watched over me. Now, instead of floating away the radiance came closer, enveloping me in a warm, pulsating luminosity and unconditional love. I no longer felt alone. I felt held.

I was ready to go.

CHAPTER 3

It's true what they say—that when you're dying your life plays out before your eyes. Mine was a slow demise. This was not my first brush with death, although until this moment I had always felt invincible.

I had begun my career working as a newspaper photographer in San Diego. Often, I crossed over the border into Mexico, photographing orphanages and the dire plight of children living in this so-called foreign country right in my own backyard.

One day, while still working at the newspaper, I was thumbing through a magazine and found myself mesmerized by the pools of light reflecting in the eyes of the Indian children staring at me from its pages. I called the photographer to tell him how much I loved his photographs. "I work for UNICEF," he said. "It sounds like the kind of work that you might be interested in. If you're ever in New York, come by and show me your portfolio." I bought a plane ticket and went to see him the following week. After looking at my photos, he asked me if I wanted to go to Nepal to photograph children there. It was exactly what I wanted to do.

My life in Nepal began in 1988 with what was supposed to be a monthlong assignment. I ended up staying there for more than four years. Working as a photographer for various relief associations and producing books and magazine articles, I became captivated by the magic of Asia. Every morning, even before opening my eyes, I'd wake up and think, "This is exactly what I want to be doing, exactly where I want to be living."

From the moment I arrived in Nepal, I felt I'd come home. My job entailed trekking to different areas of the country, but as a base I rented the top floor of a family home in Hadigau, an old pottery village in Kathmandu. My bedroom had French doors that opened onto a balcony overlooking thriving rice paddies and verdant hillsides, which were rimmed by rainbows during the summer monsoon rains.

Life was basic, but Kathmandu was an appealing place to live in the mid-1980s with a unique and interesting tight-knit expat community. True, you couldn't find clean drinking water, but you could get your legs waxed for a dollar. There were more TVs in the city than toilets. A bacteria-free green salad was unobtainable, but you could buy practically any paperback that had ever been printed.

At the time the country was locked in trade disputes with India that cut off the supply of goods and petrol. We had to make shopping runs to Thailand just to buy soap and shampoo. I bought a bright red Chinese girl's bike (Hero brand) and, like everyone else at the time, rode it wherever I went throughout the blossoming valley.

In my initial four years of living in Nepal (I continued to live there off and on over the years), I came to understand the challenges this ancient nation faced. While a small percentage of the country had become wealthy via corruption, smuggling, and an immense amount of foreign aid, most of the people in this agricultural society remained at poverty level, earning less than $160 a year. Nepali families average seven children, and at the time 20 percent of those children were expected to die before they reached the age of five. Adulthood came quickly, and child labor was rampant, especially in the carpet factories and tea fields. All these elements added up, and at the time Nepal was rated the second-poorest country in the world. People were fed up and finally took to the streets to voice their protests, demanding political and economic change.

Despite the fact that I had a friend visiting, I was out at dawn on the morning of April 6, 1990, photographing the demonstrators who, at this early hour, were already marching through the backstreets of Chetrapati and the tourist areas of Thamel. Young men in a frenzy yelled democratic slogans through bandanna-covered mouths, some waving the flag of the Nepali Congress

Party, others displaying the communist hammer and sickle. I had an assignment to photograph the ongoing protests, and I wanted to get a feeling of what was going on in the streets. I told my houseguest I'd probably be back by lunchtime.

By midmorning I was on a borrowed mountain bike, climbing the hill to Patan, amid an astonishing crowd of more than fifty thousand people marching toward the local police station. After weeks of sporadic violence, the crowd was now demonstrating calmly in public, and there was a buoyant feeling of camaraderie in the air. Incredibly, as the demonstrators passed the police and soldiers, all paused to smile and shake hands with one another. It seemed that the weeks of conflict might actually be resolved peacefully. I felt like a witness to the history of this small but significant country in the making.

By late afternoon I had positioned myself on top of the local mosque to photograph the crowds that had congregated across the street in Ratna Park. A wall of police and soldiers protecting the palace butted themselves against the growing mass of two hundred thousand. The undulating mob was approaching the king's palace as if determined to shout their slogans directly into the ears of the ruling monarchy.

Suddenly, something changed. The hands of demonstrators, which only moments before had reached out in peace, were now angrily tearing down metal signs that for so many years had paid homage to the king and the Rana family. A police booth was torn from its roots and rolled through the crowd toward the line of positioned military police in the popular public square of Durbar Marg. The air was charged; it was getting ugly. I didn't like it, yet the more the crowd became enraged, the more determined I was to get closer to the action. I climbed down from my viewpoint on top of the mosque and ran through the backstreets until I came up behind the staunch police barricade. I was determined to break through the wall of uniformed police in order to photograph the unruly scene, and I dropped down on my hands and knees, crawling between their legs.

Moving through air that was now thick with anticipation, I swung around to photograph a young boy who had managed to climb to the top of the statue of King Mahendra in front of the palace. He had grabbed the scepter from the king's iron fist and was waving it victoriously. His was a short-lived conquest; the police immediately shot him to the ground.

This set off both police and demonstrators alike, and I was now at the core of it. Police suddenly charged with *lathis*, or batons, and the crowd retaliated by throwing bottles and stones. Pushing my way through, I felt the force of a heavy stick come down on the back of my head. I tasted blood. My first reflex was to lean forward and protect my equipment, but I quickly flipped back in fright as a gun loudly went off in my face. It was only tear gas, but at extremely close range, and I was left completely incapacitated.

I immediately fell to my knees, vomiting. My head felt as if it had turned to liquid, with snot, tears, and blood running down my face in a steady flow. I threw my shirt over my nose and mouth and ran away from the line of police, my feet barely touching the ground. Once I could breathe again, the shirt came down and the camera back up. I turned around and returned into the throng, briefly noting the absurdity of a profession that obliges one to rush toward the danger that everyone else is trying to escape.

Once I was again viewing the mayhem through my lens I felt invincible. I worked my way through the horde, photographing young children pinned in doorways, their small arms raised in terror against the police batons coming down on their heads. Men and women lay on the ground, hands pressed together in the traditional namaste gesture as they pleadingly locked eyes with the soldiers and begged for mercy. The enraged military opened fire as people attempted to flee; some were shot in the back as they ran. With no ambulances allowed near the scene, the bloody bodies were dragged and carried to nearby Bir Hospital. My own eyes felt as though they had been seared with hot pokers. (Later, I was to find that they had been severely burned by the tear gas.)

At one point, I felt someone grab my shoulders from behind and pull me into the Star Hotel near Ratna Park.

"Hide your film; they're after you," whispered the Nepali teenager who worked in the hotel. He beckoned me to hide behind a wooden desk in the lobby. Seconds later, the hotel was overrun with baton-wielding police, shattering windows, mirrors, and furniture in their wake. I feared they would hear my chest pounding, yet dared to peek around the corner of the desk. Horrified, I watched as they threw open a bathroom door, where a young rickshaw driver was urinating. Dragging him by the hair to the middle of the lobby, they mercilessly began to beat him before moving on to another room. Outraged by such unprovoked violence, I ran out to comfort him. His eyes were already blindly swollen, protruding from his brutally ravished face.

Back outside, the quiet was surprising—and disconcerting. The once immense crowd looked as though it had melted into the ground. Hundreds of shoes and sandals, abandoned by their owners, now lined the empty streets, the only reminders of the violence that had taken place there.

Somehow, I managed to get back to my bike and drop my color transparency film off at a local lab, where I knew it would be safe. But the sounds of gunfire were getting louder as I rode back toward town. Where was it coming from? And at whom was it directed? I quickly returned to Ratna Park. The bamboo-shield-bearing police had now been replaced by the Nepalese Gurkha army and military soldiers (as opposed to military police), each man maneuvering behind bulletproof plastic, and they were shooting real bullets. I knelt down alongside the soldiers and began photographing them. There was no time to register emotion as I swung my camera to follow the bullets and see what they were shooting at. It was like a firing squad: the army shot directly into the crowds trapped by barricades.

Fires burned in dumpsters, sending acrid black smoke billowing into the air. Dozens of bodies lay in the street, and people were frantically carrying the wounded through the hospital doors.

Ironically, many were being shot right in front of the hospital. "Hey," hissed a small boy in Nepali, calling out from under the metal door of his storefront, "don't stay out there!" It was the first time I noticed how totally alone I was.

An older man grabbed me by the arm and pulled me toward the hospital entrance, screaming at me in Nepali: "We have your friend in here!" I didn't know if I was quite ready for what I imagined would be an intensely gruesome scene, but the man was unrelenting. "We have your friend; your friend is here!" I thought of all the boys I knew who were out demonstrating this morning, laughing with me as they waved their red flags. Was it one of them?

The scene in the hospital resembled a battlefield. Bodies lined the floor shoulder to shoulder throughout the lobby and into the next room. Torn T-shirts had been wrapped around various appendages as crude bandages. My dirty boots tracked bloody imprints as I moved from person to person. It was obvious that the small hospital staff had far more patients than they could handle. The man who led me in tugged on my arm. "Your friend, your friend," he whispered.

A doctor approached us. "Do you know him?" he asked. I looked down. Blue eyes caked with blood stared back at me. A Westerner had been killed, obviously a tourist. There was a clean bullet hole right in his jugular.

"No. I don't know. I'm not sure," I stammered. Actually, he looked very familiar, like the friend who was visiting me. Had he worried about me and ventured out of the house? His features were so bloodied it was difficult to tell.

"We need to find out who he is." The doctor looked at me apologetically. "And as you can see we're really quite overwhelmed."

Coincidentally, I had interviewed the doctor a couple of days earlier when the staff had staged a protest at the hospital. He now encouraged me to photograph as many of the bodies as soon as possible. "Especially the Western guy. Police trucks are gathering the dead bodies from here and in the streets. We don't know where they're taking them. We hear they may be dumping them in a mass grave out near Gorkhana Park. We'll never know how many people have really been killed today. Bastards."

In what felt like a truly sacred act, I knelt down and opened the money belt resting against the young man's bony hips. There I found a typical traveler's stash: a few rupees, Drum tobacco, rolling papers, travel documents. My heart ached as I thought of his poor parents. Pulling out his British passport, I shakily read his name and birth date to the doctor. Only twenty-six years old, he was indeed a tourist. We were about the same age and the same nationality—I had dual citizenship, with both U.S. and British passports. I thought, "What on earth were you doing out in the middle of this mess?" as I closed up his money belt. I looked around and asked myself the same question.

Another tourist caught in the crossfire arrived, with his leg shattered by a bullet below the knee. The doctors told me that the army had been shooting illegal dumdum bullets, which splinter upon impact and had been banned under international law since 1945. If they could get him to Bangkok within six hours they might be able to save his leg. But with the imposed twenty-four-hour curfew, the airport was closed, and the doctors proceeded to amputate his leg then and there, in the dingy Bir Hospital in Kathmandu.

I ran back out to where I'd stashed my bike and rapidly pedaled back up the street to the photo lab. Five intimidating soldiers blocked the road, pointing their sinister-looking guns at eye level. I knew from what I'd just seen that they weren't kidding.

"There's a curfew, you know, and you shouldn't be on the streets," one told me severely.

"A curfew? Oh, okay," I said, trying to sound calm. "My hotel is up here. I'm staying at the Yak 'n Yeti," I lied.

As I cycled through town, I kept swinging my blonde hair, praying that the lost tourist bit would carry me through town safely. They were surprised to see me at the Associated Press office, but pleased to have some black-and-white film, which, unlike color, could be sent out over the newswire.

There was no way I could get back to my house through the roadblocks, so instead I headed to the tourist area of Thamel and checked in at the Shambhala Hotel. I was just glad to be in a place that served cold beer. The roof garden took on a surreal quality compared to what I had just witnessed. A couple playing backgammon in the corner passed a sweet-smelling joint back and forth. Now stuck in their hotels indefinitely, the tourists were accommodating themselves to having their travel plans interrupted by a political upheaval.

The next morning, above the objections of my friends who worked at the hotel, I sneaked out on my bicycle during curfew. Stopping at the hospital, I was amazed to see a now empty hallway. Seems it had been a slow night: after the city was closed off, no one had been allowed to bring in the injured.

The town was empty except for gun-toting soldiers and the army tanks crawling along the outer Ring Road of Kathmandu city. Taking a chance, I rode my bike at top speed out to the airport where tourists were lined up waiting to escape. After some serious pleading, I convinced a man heading to India to carry my film out in his sock, where a representative from *Time* magazine would meet him and pick it up.

On a television broadcast that evening, the king announced that he would meet with the democratic party leaders to discuss the possibility of introducing a prime minister into the current government. He then proceeded to lift the curfew. Tragically, he neglected to inform the police on duty. As cheering celebrants ran into the streets, they were promptly shot. And the nation continued to simmer in its desire for a better way of life.

Most photojournalists rely on a rush of adrenaline to keep thinking on their feet and get through a dire situation. We cover these stories because they matter to us and hope they will to other people. But some of us admit that, later, in the quiet moments, we sometimes go back to the hotel and have a good cry. We weep for the suffering of others, the injustice, the inconceivability that such pure good and blatant evil can exist in the world. We feel frustration for our own inability to make things right. We pray that our risks and imagery will make even some small impact in the lives we touch and create something positive. We cling to the dream that we might actually make a difference in the world.

With a camera held up in front of my face I always felt untouchable, that despite potential danger I could move through situations like these ensconced in a protective bubble. "If you're not living on the edge, you're taking up too much room," I used to laugh with my friends. There was no closer edge than lying eviscerated on that roadside.

Now, as I lay on the wooden bed in Laos, gasping for my last breath of life, I realized that my bubble had finally burst.

And all I had done was simply get on a bus.

CHAPTER 4

I don't know how much time elapsed; it might have been minutes or it might have been hours. Someone took my hand, and I awoke to the lilt of an unfamiliar English accent.

"Alison, wake up, wake up." I was far away at this point, surrendering to what I hoped would be a peaceful death. I was swathed in a warm white light and no longer felt any pain. I desperately did not want to return. (I imagine this is what a baby feels before being slammed into the harsh reality of cold and brightness.) But all of a sudden I was outside my body, looking down on it. And then the steely pain returned, resounding throughout my nerve endings. My throat and mouth were so dry I could manage only short, labored breaths through my nose.

I was back. Apparently it wasn't my time to go.

The voice belonged to Alan, a British aid worker whose breath reeked of whiskey. He had discovered my passport and was calling my name. Alan told me he lived in Kasi with his wife, Van. I found out later that they had started their own local relief organization, which among other things detonated mines and bombs left behind from the Vietnam War. More important to me at the moment, they had a truck. "I'm going to get you help," he said. His plan was to drive the 150 miles south to the capital of Vientiane, where he could get an ambulance.

I looked at him weakly and mouthed, "There's not time." He took my hand, looked into my eyes, and told me that he knew I was right. It was 7:00 P.M. I'd been lying there injured for more than six hours.

"Okay," he said. "I'm going to take you in my vehicle." He warned me, with a bit of a chuckle, that because it was the New Year, he'd been drinking all day.

What was I going to do, wait for the next ride? "Just get me out of here," I whispered.

With the help of the other men, Alan and Van lifted me in my straw-mat stretcher and gently placed me in the back of their pickup truck. I was unable to lie flat, so I rested my head on the hard metal hump of the wheel well. For the next seven hours, my broken bones jarred against the metal ribbing of the truck bed as we slowly maneuvered over heavily potholed roads toward Vientiane.

Roel and Meia had come along too and were in the front of the truck. Roel periodically called out in his Dutch accent, "Alison, you still all right?" I mumbled a response. I was so grateful for his presence and for his continued concern.

"Bless your heart," Alan told me later, "you didn't say a word the whole time." Instead I focused on a sky full of stars, certain it would be the last thing I would see in this lifetime. How beautiful they were. I felt that I wasn't alone, that I was being watched over, that I was a part of something much bigger. Was this the end, I wondered? And would there be something of my spirit to live on? I felt there would be. I still wasn't sure I was going to make it, but I felt a total trust in the universe, whichever way it was going to go.

I am not a card-carrying devotee, but from my years of studying Eastern philosophy I have found that Buddhism, with its emphasis on wisdom and compassion, makes the most sense to me of all the religions. I was first introduced to *vipassanā,* a Buddhist meditation practice, while living in Nepal. The retreats I attended in different parts of Asia offered a much-needed respite when my speeding train of life threatened to disrail. For up to three weeks at a time I have sat with monks in the coconut groves of Thailand, the forests of Burma, and monasteries in Nepal, Tibet, India, and even California.

In the back of that truck, I found myself relying on the meditation technique I'd learned during those retreats. I was intently focusing on my breathing in order to control the intense pain and to stay conscious. I didn't cry out in anguish. I now turned inward. We are often surrounded by physical discomfort, but I had discovered that if we plant ourselves in the stillness long enough, even pain will pass. The fact that it was so difficult to breathe made it even more important that I not panic. Slowly inhale, slowly exhale. What a delicate pearl each savored breath becomes when you think another may not follow. A single wisp of air, the last thing each of us will leave on the planet.

Living among the twenty-five-hundred-year-old Buddhist cultures in Asia has influenced my belief that our energy doesn't die; something in our inner soul or spirit lives on.

Many years ago I visited the Tibetan community in Darjeeling, India, with a Tibetan friend. We traveled into the hills with the intent of meeting Kalu Rinpoche. He had once been the tutor to the young Dalai Lama, but by the time we went to meet him he was a very old man, and ill. A cold rain fell as we waited outside his monastery home. After some time his caretaker came out.

"I'm sorry," he said, "but Kalu Rinpoche is too ill to see you." Sadly, he died just a few months later.

Years passed, and then I heard that the reincarnation of Kalu Rinpoche had been discovered and was visiting in Dharamsala. Coincidentally, I was there to attend some of the Dalai Lama's teaching sessions, and I decided to go visit the young boy where he was staying at the Norbulingka monastery. When I arrived, his mother led me to his room, left me outside, and I heard her tell him who I was and that I wanted to photograph him. Through the door I heard him complaining about the intrusion, and as I entered he looked up distractedly from his Game Boy. Then he astounded me:

40

"I remember you," he said, brightening. "You came to visit me in Darjeeling. It was raining. My caretaker was making *momo* dumplings. I was too ill to see you then, but I'll see you now."

As I lay in the back of the truck I thought of that reincarnation, and though at the time I'd been amazed by it, now it simply gave me reassurance.

My mind drifted to a dinner I'd had with friends in Nepal six weeks earlier. My friend insisted that his female companion had a knack for fortune-telling. "Go on, then," I said laughing, thrusting my hand toward her, while holding a glass of wine in the other. Laying my palm flat, the woman predicted that I would be in a terrible car accident. "That's an awful thing to tell me," I said, snapping my hand back from hers.

"I'm sorry, it's just so pronounced," she told me. It felt strange to be living out this premonition. But I remembered that she'd also said I would be all right. And that gave me hope.

After a few hours the truck stopped in the town of Vang Vieng, which had been my original destination when I boarded the bus. It was late at night, but Alan managed to find a nurse, who gave me an injection of Panadol. Unfortunately, it didn't do much for the sharp grinding in my numerous broken bones. Each one still screamed in agony, and there was no way I could get comfortable.

"I'm sorry, but that's the extent of what I can do here," the nurse told us. She had never dealt with such severe injuries and encouraged us to carry on toward the capital. Alan had a car radiophone and begged someone from the U.S. embassy in Vientiane to come and meet us. My heart sank when I heard them deny his request, admitting that even they were intimidated by the recent attacks on the roads.

"Listen, I've got a woman in the back of my truck with a broken back and collapsed lungs, and it's going to be on your shoulders when you have to deal with a dead American," he said. Thankfully, his scare tactics worked. A few hours later, two representatives from the embassy met our vehicle on the side of the road. I was never so glad to hear an American accent in my life.

They were not very hopeful once they saw me. "Were you riding on the roof?" one asked. "We see so much of this here, but you're by far the worst." The embassy officials, Joseph and Michael, explained that the medical facilities in Vientiane were extremely limited, so the new plan was to get me to Thailand, which was about another two-hour drive south. They would need to open the Thai-Lao Friendship Bridge, which was closed for the night, in order for me to cross over from Laos into Thailand. Meanwhile they took my brother's phone number so they could contact him.

Finally, I was transferred to an ambulance. I was surprised to find that the vehicle was brand new. As I was its first passenger, I requested the siren for this inaugural ride. There was an extremely kind Australian doctor on board. Ironically, Joe Cummings had told me about him when we were together in Luang Prabang. Joe had said that he only helped Australians, and I joked with the doctor faintly, asking if that were true.

"I guess if you're this bad we can help you Americans out once in a while," he laughed. He placed me on a backboard and in a neck brace, which seemed a little futile after all the jostling I'd been through. For years I'd wanted to see Vientiane, but in my wildest dreams I'd never imagined it would be from the back of an ambulance at night.

Once over the bridge and into Thailand, I was met by a paramedic and transferred to a second ambulance, which drove me yet another two hours to the Aek Udon International Hospital—a military medical institution from the days of the Vietnam War—in Udon Thani in northeastern Thailand.

It was three in the morning when I arrived, fourteen hours after the crash. I was alive. But barely. Though I should have been dead, by some small miracle I was still breathing.

CHAPTER 5

"Another two hours and you wouldn't be alive," Dr. Bunsom Santithamnont told me in heavily accented English.

In yet another stroke of good fortune, Dr. Bunsom, as he introduced himself, happened to be a respected surgeon and a recent transfer from Bangkok to Udon Thani. He was also the only doctor on call. When he met the stretcher he was incredulous that I had survived such intensive injuries, but as he read my X-rays his face clouded.

All the ribs on my left side had snapped like pencils. I had a pneumothorax, a collapsed left lung that had filled with fluid and blood, and my diaphragm was punctured, which explained my difficulty breathing. My spleen was lacerated; my back, pelvis, and coccyx were broken. The doctor had not been able to get a breathing tube into my chest, and now we learned the reason: all my internal organs, including my heart, my intestines, and even my bowels had been torn loose and were smashed up into my right shoulder. What an image—I didn't even know they could do that. Listening to this litany, I somehow managed to quietly plead, "Please don't take out anything unless you really have to."

To my dismay, I was allowed no painkillers, as they could compromise my already limited breathing. As Dr. Bunsom prepped me for emergency surgery, I noticed Roel on the phone from across the room.

It seems that the U.S. embassy had put through a call to my brother, leaving an urgent message to call back. "Your sister has been in a terrible car crash. We have her in a hospital in Udon Thani, Thailand. You better catch the first flight here. It doesn't look good. She's in critical condition, and we think she might not make it."

"That's the message you really want to hear on the machine when you walk in the door," my brother told Roel when he called back. I felt great comfort in knowing there was now a connection to someone I knew and loved. "He wants to know if you can move your feet," Roel called over to me.

Roel looked over, and then informed him that, yes, I could wiggle my toes.

"Good. He says you're probably not paralyzed."

My new Dutch friend nervously bounced back and forth between me and his girlfriend, who was being treated in the next bed. Meia had a broken arm and a bad concussion. She remembered nothing from the accident, fortunately. I, on the other hand, had every single moment seared into my memory as if in slow motion. When I closed my eyes I could still see the look of terror on the people's faces as they anticipated the impact, the glass shattering, the vivid screams, and I recalled the way all the air was punched from my body, as if I were on a roller coaster that slammed into a wall. I was so desperately tired: overcome with the sheer exhaustion of the memories and the effort of trying to stay alive.

"Can I take a photo of you?" Roel asked. "I've never seen anyone look so peaceful before." The photo shows my lacerated arm, my hair damp with sweat and blood. My eyes were dark and dilated, already deep in another world. I was in shock. As I was wheeled in for surgery, I reminded Roel to give my good-bye note to my brother.

"Give it to him yourself," he said with a smile, and laid a comforting hand on my shoulder.

It was such a relief when the anesthesia mask was placed over my face. Finally, I could hand myself over, stop struggling, and welcome sleep.

And then, I flatlined.

Dr. Bunsom, having never done a procedure this complicated before, immediately cut my chest cavity open down to the pubic bone, and in a lifesaving race against time pulled my damaged ribs apart and managed to untangle my organs. He sutured my lungs and diaphragm and was able to finally wedge a breathing tube down my throat. As per my earlier request, he left in my spleen. I didn't know what a spleen did, I just knew that, along with all my other organs, I wanted it. He managed to stop me from bleeding to death on the table. With the greatest of care he massaged and revived the essence of my being. This is a man who has literally held my heart in his hands.

I spent the next couple of days unconscious in intensive care. In a moment of vague wakefulness, I was surprised to find Jerry Alexander, the photographer I had met on New Year's Eve in Laos, gently rubbing my feet. Soothing music played from the portable CD headset he had placed on my ears. I thought I was dreaming. I was on a ventilator and unable to talk.

Jerry brought me a notebook, and I scribbled, "How?"

"The nurses found Oliver's business card in your pocket and called his gallery. He ran down the main street of Luang Prabang calling for me. I immediately flew down here." I was moved by the compassionate gesture that someone I had just met and barely knew would come all the way to Thailand to make sure I wasn't alone when I woke up from surgery.

Our friend Joe Cummings arrived shortly afterward and helped by acting as an interpreter between me and the doctors. As he sat by my bed, he cracked open the Lonely Planet guidebook I'd been holding when the crash happened. Chunks of glass fell from its blood-splattered pages. "Thanks for giving me something to write about when I upgrade this," he teased. "I think we'll try selling yours on eBay."

I was touched by everyone's kindness. I felt so weak, so vulnerable—trapped in a cavern of unbearable pain. Even the air around me hurt my body. I continued to dip in and out of consciousness. Unable to breathe on my own, I was hooked up to a respirator.

My brother, Andrew, flew to Thailand a few days later. When he entered the intensive care unit dressed in the mandatory pea green scrubs, a big smile spread across my face, and the machinery immediately began to beep and come to life.

"That made it worth the whole trip," Andrew said, returning my smile.

CHAPTER 6

As only siblings, Andrew and I were extremely close, although our lives were so busy we didn't get to see each other as often as we would have liked. I was always on the road, and he was busy raising a family, living with his wife and two (soon to be three) children in Denver. The time he spent in the hospital, sleeping at the foot of my bed, was the most time we'd spent together in our adult lives.

Andrew has visited me wherever I have lived, all over the world, but never under such extreme circumstances. When the American embassy called him about my accident, he didn't hesitate to jump on a plane to come and help me, despite his second daughter, Hannah, having been born just two months before. "I had to look up Udon Thani on the Internet to find out where on earth it was," he said with a grin.

As he placed them at my bedside, I was touched that he had taken the time to comb the racks at the airport and bring every trashy gossip magazine he could find. With tubes protruding from all points of my body, I could see it was a shock for him to realize that I was being kept alive by machines and it would be quite a while before I would be able to wrap my mind around even such basic reading material.

I watched as my younger brother unpacked the bags of Tootsie Rolls, Goldfish crackers, Peppermint Patties, and Keebler cookies that he had brought as sustenance for the trip. He is not a big fan of foreign food. "Twizzlers," he taunted, waving my favorite in front of my face, knowing full well I couldn't eat them. After feeling so traumatized and disoriented I found great comfort in these small but familiar gestures.

With my one functioning arm, I communicated by scribbling notes on a pad kept at my bedside.

"I'm so glad you're here," I wrote.

Joe and Andrew met daily with Dr. Bunsom for updates on my condition.

"She is one lucky girl. And strong," Dr. Bunsom had told them in impressive English. "The internal injuries were our first concern. I was shocked when I went in and saw how much internal bleeding there was. Given that, I was amazed that she survived for so long. I initially went in and sewed up her lungs and diaphragm, so that she will eventually be able to breathe on her own, although we won't know for some time how much lung capacity is lost. We're trying to drain the fluids from them now. I had to move her heart and intestines back into place, as they were compressing her lungs and compromising her breathing as well. Her spleen was lacerated, but we left it in, and hopefully it will heal. We'll find out if her bladder works once we take the catheter out."

Dr. Bunsom showed them X-rays of the damage.

"All the ribs on the left side are broken and twisted, but we have to leave them to mend on their own. They should eventually reconnect. There are breaks to the tailbone, the pelvis, and the back. It appears that these breaks aren't paralyzing. Again, very lucky. If the break in the lower sacrum had been even a few centimeters over it would be a very different story. I think she will walk again; I just don't know how well. These things take time, a lot of time." A severe aubergine-colored bruise had spread down the whole left side of my body, which bore an actual indent from the impact of the truck.

"We have been performing a number of operations to remove much of the glass and metal left in her arm," the doctor added. "And we're trying to make sure we combat infection, as the initial surgery wasn't performed under the best conditions."

"He's not kidding," I scrawled after Andrew sat down and relayed to me the doctor's prognosis of the numerous surgeries I'd had so far.

*　　*　　*

With his blond hair and good looks, Andrew was an immediate hit with the giggling Thai nurses. I suspected he might have been the reason they checked up on me so often. Whatever the case, the medical staff certainly did their best to make sure I was as comfortable and content as possible during my three weeks in the hospital. The nurses were all incredibly sweet, except for the one who kept elevating and lowering my bed at an alarming rate. Unable to speak through my ventilator, I made the sign of a cross with my fingers whenever she came near me.

One day she came in and began rinsing my parched mouth with mouthwash. I hadn't been able to drink fluids all week, and I was dreaming of how good a Sprite would taste. Suddenly, her fingers pushed roughly against my respirator, setting off my gag reflex. I began to choke. In a panic I grabbed my pad and scribbled, "I can't breathe, I can't breathe, take this tube out!" Terrified, I frantically grabbed at my throat with one hand while waving my notepad to get Jerry's attention with the other. Just then the doctor walked in and quickly yanked the respirator from my throat. I promptly threw up. At least I was now off the ventilator. And I was breathing on my own.

Now that I could talk, Andrew and I spent long hours sharing updates of our lives and memories from our childhood, something we had never had the time to do before. I knew it was difficult for my family to understand my lifestyle, and they had long been concerned about my well-being while traveling so much. Now their worst nightmare had come true.

* * *

It seems that I developed my wanderlust while still in utero.

My mother was a British flight attendant, working for Pan Am, when she met my father. He was a research chemist from Belgium who had played rugby while at the University of Cambridge. She fell in love with his legs, and he fell in love with hers. It may not have been the best basis for a marriage, but they wed in England and relocated to America.

Given my mother's profession, travel was part of my life from the time I was an infant, and I obtained my first passport while still sucking a pacifier. I even had a special bassinet to fly in. Mom always knew the pilots, so when I got a little older I could sit on their laps in the cockpit and watch the world below.

Once my brother was old enough, my mother would take us to Newark airport as a recreational activity. We'd sit on the hood of the car, eating long straps of black licorice, and watch the planes take off. I loved the smell of jet fuel.

As a family, we often flew back to Europe to visit relatives. Mom strode through airports with confidence and, like all the other women at the time, wore stilettos and furs and smelled of perfume and cigarettes. I was exhilarated by the exotic and the unfamiliar as people chattered in strange languages. I received my first camera for Christmas when I was ten years old and fell in love with taking pictures. My little Kodak Instamatic went everywhere with me, and photographing people helped me overcome my innate shyness. It became a key to the door of other people's lives.

Dad was the cerebral anchor of the family, earning two doc-torates in his days at Cambridge: one in physics and the other in chemistry. My father was much more comfortable with his books than with people, and when he did speak, it was with a distinctive British accent. Dad always sported a silk ascot, even while mow-ing the lawn. It was an unusual look for the suburbs of New Jersey and a cause for amusement years later whenever he visited me in San Francisco.

Mom, on the other hand, was much more outgoing and loved a good party. She eventually, and very reluctantly, left the airline, became a secretary, and quickly worked her way up the corporate ladder, landing herself a high-powered position as a commodities broker. She spent more and more time at the office, working late into the evenings. Andrew and I often returned from school and entertained ourselves in the wooded area behind our home, which boasted a pond big enough for ice-skating in the winter. Mom would sometimes grow exasperated when we called and inter-rupted her at the office.

"Go down and see if the pond is frozen," she'd say. Andrew and I would run onto the ice, our small bodies causing hairline cracks to spread beneath our feet. To test if the ice would hold us, we lugged the wooden patio furniture down to the pond and sent it out on ice-floe recognizance. During the course of the winter we watched as each bench fell through the thin surface. Winter was long, and we eventually worked our way through all the cedar pic-nic benches. It wasn't until well after the snow melted that Mom came out onto the terrace with the first warm-weather platter of hamburgers to be barbecued, and demanded, "Where the hell is my patio furniture?!"

I had an insatiable desire for exploring. Even when I was young my independent streak worried my parents. I had an uncontrollable habit of wandering off. As I got a little older, my daring only grew. As teenagers, my friends and I would throw on backpacks and spend our Saturdays following rivers, fishing, and hiking through the New Jersey woods. One day I scaled a sheer rock wall in the local quarry and got stuck midway. Copperhead snakes were crawling above, and I was too daunted to climb down. In the end I had to be brought back to earth by the local rescue squad. "Please don't tell my dad," I begged them. That became my mantra throughout life.

My father simply shook his head when he read about my adventure in the local paper.

One night, when I was about fifteen, I had just returned home from an evening photography class I was taking at the local high school when my mother called us into the family room and told us she was taking a trip to San Francisco. Her company was relocating to the West Coast, and her flight was leaving that night. Although she had discussed the possibility of moving out there to follow her job, seeing her packed bags made it seem suddenly final.

"I'll be back in two weeks," she said with a wave.

She never returned.

I felt numb. I harbored the worry that in my teenage rebellion I had done something to make her leave. That first night, and for many after, Andrew, who was ten at the time, crawled into my bed and slept with me.

"Why did Mom leave?" he asked, his blond head propped up against my pillows. He was hugging his old stuffed Winnie the Pooh that had once gone everywhere with him.

"I don't know, I guess she doesn't love Dad anymore," I told him as I draped my arms around his skinny pajama-clad shoulders.

"Why not?" he persisted.

I didn't have an answer.

My father, clearly upset, did the best he could. I took over making lunches for my brother, cheering at his soccer games, and driving him around when I was old enough.

But overhearing my dad's sorrow through my bedroom walls, I resolved that I would never let anyone incapacitate me like that. From that moment on, photography and writing became more than a hobby to me. They became a lifeline.

While Andrew sought out stability, I ran in the opposite direction. At the age of sixteen, I moved into my own apartment, working as a maid in a hotel while finishing high school. I wanted my freedom.

I was fortunate that I'd had influential high school teachers who saw that I was struggling with my home life and took me under their wing. Mr. Lee, my English teacher, nurtured my love of writing and photography. He became my mentor, teaching me how to use my first real SLR camera. He taught me the impact of a good documentary photo story. "You know you can actually earn a living doing this," he told me after encouraging me to work on the school yearbook and newspaper. From the moment I heard the word *photojournalist* I knew that was what I wanted to be.

Andrew, being a younger brother, was the obvious photo target, but he has always hated having his picture taken.

"Remember how I would chase you down on the soccer and lacrosse field?" I asked him in the hospital. "I'd beg you to model in my little studio in the basement, next to where I'd set up that darkroom."

"And when you got that stupid tape recorder and kept trying to interview me."

I laughed. "Yeah, every recording basically consisted of 'Go away!' or 'Leave me alone!'"

You can't help where you were born and raised, but I knew there was something bigger out there waiting for me. The day after my high school graduation, I tied my surfboard to the roof of my bright yellow Honda and drove out to California to attend college. My father gave me a backpack as my graduation present. Years later my brother got a briefcase. We now laughed at how our fates seemed sealed even then. I learned at an early age that we have at least some control over our destiny. And now, years later, I appreciated how a little adversity can make you a stronger person in the long run. If you survive it.

*   *   *

Over the next few days, Joe, Jerry, and Andrew went over every X-ray. In fact, they were so vigilant with their questions about each subsequent surgery that it prompted Dr. Bunsom to ask them if they were doctors too. It was apparent that it wasn't the Thai custom for relatives and friends of patients to be so involved in the process. Nevertheless, the doctor patiently explained every procedure. Meanwhile, I allowed myself to be carried along. I had no choice; I couldn't seem to get my brain out of its cloudy haze.

Amazingly, all my luggage from the bus had followed me there. It was Andrew who went through my backpack and found the bloodied denim shirt and torn black pants that I'd been wearing that fateful day. He thought I wasn't watching, but I registered the emotion on his face when he saw the caked blood and blue paint from the truck ingrained in my pants and the pieces of broken glass that fell to the floor as he unrolled them. He threw the pants in the garbage and replaced them with a new pair he'd bought for me to wear when the time came to go home.

"So how's Dad holding up?" I eventually asked Andrew, my voice still hoarse from having the tube in my throat removed.

"Of course he's worried, and he wanted to come to Thailand himself. He's just not healthy enough to make it." Dad had been battling bone cancer for the last few years. "But," Andrew said to reassure me, "he's still doing the *New York Times* crossword puzzle every day—in ink."

One day Andrew came into my hospital room carrying a pot

of exquisite purple orchids he'd found for sale in the street. He opened the blinds, and specks of dust floated in the streams of sunlight. I watched him place the flowers on the windowsill and thought about how much I admired the man he had become: a stand-up guy, honest and hardworking. He was devoted to his wife, a fun and patient dad who worked hard to create the loving home he'd always wanted when growing up. I wanted to tell him how much he meant to me.

"Despite the circumstances, I'm really glad we had this time together," I said. "You're the best brother I could have asked for." I felt a wave of gratitude for having been given the opportunity to be around to tell him this. I wondered about the note I had written to him when I was sure that I was dying. I had been clutching it in my hand when I went into surgery, but someone must have taken it. Roel had been right. Now I was blessed with the chance to let Andrew, and all those around me, know how much I appreciated them. We're not always so lucky.

I thought back to a friend who had been killed in a car wreck when I was a junior in college. Another friend was driving. They were cruising down a highway, coming home late from a bar, when they were suddenly blindsided by a telephone pole. That night my departed friend came to see me: as clear as day his presence stood in my bedroom. I was left to say good-bye to an apparition. It was the first time someone so close to me had died, and I was deeply affected. I ditched classes and hibernated in my room. I couldn't fathom how someone's young life could be cut short so soon.

61

Once again a teacher cared enough to step in. My documentary photo instructor noticed how the incident was affecting me: my grades were seriously slipping. He took me aside. "You'd better pull yourself together," he reproached me severely, in an attempt to pull me out of my self-indulgent mourning. "If you're going to pursue this career, you'd better toughen up. You're going to have to endure a lot more emotional upheaval than this. People die. It's a fact of life. Get it together or you're not going to pass this year." As difficult as it was to hear his harsh words, he was right. I threw myself into my work and went from failing to the honor roll. It was an early lesson in the fragility of life and the reality of death. I watched as Andrew watered the orchids. You just never know when it might be the last time you see someone, I thought.

It was during that time in college that I first decided to travel to the developing world and began to save my money to do so.

Because of the books I'd read on Eastern philosophy, and seeing the movie *Gandhi,* I was drawn to the spiritualism of India. I wanted to break out of the confines of my small, suburban world and explore the human extreme. My father expressed his apprehension. He felt India was too far, too strange, too dangerous. He encouraged me to backpack in Europe instead. This didn't sound nearly as compelling, but I agreed.

When I got to Spain, I had someone send a series of postcards telling my family how much I was enjoying the beaches. Meanwhile, I jumped on a boat and traveled to North Africa. It was a defining experience. Those first glimpses of overwhelming poverty, of refugees and children in need, became etched in my mind, and I knew then that these were the issues I cared about most and wanted to document.

I had someone else mail my postcards raving about the beaches of Greece, while I was actually hitchhiking around the Middle East, living with bedouins in the Sinai and Egypt. I worked on a kibbutz in Israel for a few months, and when the American embassy in Beirut was bombed, I donned Israeli army fatigues and hitched rides in local army trucks to get inside the country. I was caught trying to impersonate a soldier and was briefly held in an Israeli military camp, where the commander in charge unceremoniously ripped the film from my camera. I was eventually sent back across the border, but my quest for adventure was just beginning. Working my way around the world for that year boosted my self-confidence. I was twenty-one and I was fearless.

And now I could barely take a breath. Four times a day I had to blow into a handheld plastic device to strengthen my lung capacity. The small colored balls inside of it were supposed to be pushed upward with each exhalation.

I could never get those balls to budge. "This is broken," I'd tell Andrew in frustration and hand it over to him. He'd give a mighty blow, and with a ping they'd hit the top of the device. Passing it back, he'd encourage me to try again.

CHAPTER 7

It was a day of celebration when I was finally moved out of intensive care and into my own room. Udon Thani was a modern-enough town that Andrew was able to duck out to the local 7-Eleven and buy me a congratulatory frozen Coke. After having a tube down my throat for so long, it tasted divine.

It seemed surreal to watch the familiar face of the comedian Jay Leno in the evenings on the television Dr. Bunsom had personally hooked up for me. I found Leno especially funny while stoned on the huge quantities of drugs I was taking. I have dim memories of watching a movie called *Fearless*, in which the survivor of a plane crash subsequently feels invincible and takes numerous risks with his life. He feels nothing can kill him after this survival experience. I, on the other hand, just lay there feeling broken and fragile.

Drug-induced dreams haunted me for weeks. Reliving the accident jolted me out of sleep with such force that the bed jumped, sending the nurses into laughter. But what I remember most about those long days and nights is never being able to get enough pain relief from my self-regulating morphine drip. Dr. Bunsom was keeping a close eye on my intake of opiates. He had seen too many addicts pass through Thai hospitals.

I was no stranger to hospitals; my body had already withstood some pretty extreme health issues during my travels. Living with the locals, eating their food and drinking their water, had brought me numerous bouts of dysentery and giardia, as well as typhoid, dengue fever, malaria, hepatitis, and countless worms.

After living in Asia for several years, my body became badly weakened, to the point where I was unable to digest food properly. I went to see a doctor, David Shlim, who was a favorite with the expats, at a health clinic in Kathmandu. He was a devout Buddhist and known for his gentle nature and his discretion, considering he knew so many intimate details about the people in the close community. At his advice I eventually left Nepal, infected by a mysterious new disease that the clinic had labeled "blue-green algae." I flew to London, where I was treated for three months at the Hospital for Tropical Diseases.

Although I was seen mostly as an outpatient, I was admitted for about a week. It was a fascinating stay. I shared nightly dinners with people from all over the world, and we tried to top one another with the bizarreness of our ailments.

There was the uptight businessman who had been bitten by a tick in Africa and whose leg had swollen to the size of a tree trunk. One time I bumped into a man in a wheelchair as I was coming out of the bathroom. "Whoa, what happened to you?" I blurted, taken aback by his disfigured face. He looked as though he were melting; he had no nose and part of his ear was missing. "Oh, some spice I ate in India," he said through his drooping mouth. I knew leprosy when I saw it.

"He doesn't want anyone to know because of the social stigma," a nurse later took me aside and explained. "It's not as highly infectious as people think. It's easily detected and certainly curable. Poor guy must have harbored it for quite some time for it to be this advanced."

During that week, I shared a room with a young woman who had lived in Africa more than a decade earlier. One day, after all those years while looking in the mirror as she brushed her hair, she saw a worm crawl across her eyeball. She performed a fabulously entertaining reenactment of her disgust at pulling this vile creature from her eye. An English guy down the hall suffered from the same thing. The treatment for this disease, loa loa filariasis, is extraordinary: blood is drawn, centrifuged, and put back in the body—the patient is also given a slew of antibiotics. The Englishman showed me how the worms then popped up dead: small fossil-like, crescent-shaped creatures pressing through his skin.

I retaliated by showing him the results of my jejunum test. In order to try to identify my disease, I'd had to swallow a string while the other end was taped to the outside of my mouth. The hope was that the parasites would cling to the line and thereby be able to be studied; but the next morning, as the nurse pulled the string all the way through my intestine, all I saw was sludgy green bile and muck. She dropped it into a jar, but at least I had a good use for it: I raced to show it to my new loa loa friends. Presenting my disgusting trophy, I was the winner that day.

I was eventually diagnosed with a newly discovered parasite now called cyclospora. Given how sick it made me, my doctors told me I should avoid Asia for a while. For once, I took their advice and headed back to the United States. I thought graduate school would be good idea, as it would also offer me the ongoing health care I would need.

I attended the University of California at Berkeley, where I wrote my thesis on visual anthropology, the concept of using photography and film to learn about distant cultures. Along with my thesis, I concluded my studies with an exhibit of my Tibet photographs, introducing the idea of visual anthropology to the Phoebe A. Hearst Museum of Anthropology. I graduated in 1993, which was also the year I received the Dorothea Lange Fellowship in Documentary Photography to continue my project of documenting child labor in Asia. I left the university with diploma in hand, a book contract under my belt, and, most important, a healthy body. Or so I thought.

Shortly after graduating I was back in Nepal, and it took no time at all for something else to go wrong. I was photographing the trek from Gokyo Lake to Mount Everest, and scrambling across the 17,780-foot, scree-covered Cho La pass had been exhausting. It was not a welcome discovery to find the next morning that my eye was nearly swollen shut by a golf ball–size lump that had formed just above it. A doctor on the trip advised me to get an X-ray as soon as possible.

"It could be cancer," he said. Not the suggestion I'd hoped for while atop a remote Himalayan mountain.

Back in Kathmandu, I went to see David Shlim at the clinic. He was already highly acclaimed in the medical world for his findings on cyclospora, so he was excited to see the large round mass above my eye. Unfortunately, its presence was elusive. It seemed to have a life of its own, coming up in the middle of the night or at high altitude. He didn't have an answer, and I didn't pursue it any further.

Months later, on a layover in Bangkok, the symptoms made a dramatic reappearance, and I decided to visit an emergency room. Peering into my eye, the doctor seemed to know what was going on right away.

"You have gnathosomiasis," he announced. "It's a worm that grows under the skin, and yours is quite big. You must have had it for some time. We'll do a blood test, but there's only a fifty percent chance that it will show up positive, as it comes up only at certain times, for feeding."

69

"Feeding? Feeding on what?"

"Well, it lives in your soft tissues and feeds on nutrients in your blood. The usual remedy is to surgically remove it, although if you decide not to, the average life span of these worms is only about ten years."

He went on to explain that I could have gotten the worm from eating undercooked shellfish here in Thailand. The host is usually a cat; it was unusual for the worm to park itself in the head of a human. I had expected a sinus infection. Maybe even a brain tumor. But a worm living in my head? This was definitely one of those times when I lamented the fact that I hadn't settled down to get married, have kids, and live in suburbia. Sure enough, my blood test was positive, but because of my heavy travel schedule I didn't do anything right away. Besides, I really wasn't keen on the idea of someone burrowing into my head. The lump would appear so sporadically that I would be concerned when it showed up but mostly forget about it when it didn't.

One day it made one of its rare appearances and I decided to go see Dr. Shlim again. "Look, I've got this five pounds I just can't lose," I joked. There happened to be a doctor, Marty Cetron from the Centers for Disease Control, visiting from Atlanta that day, and he was incredulous when he heard I'd had this for nearly two years.

"What, are you crazy? That thing is working its way toward your brain. You have to get that removed right away. Come to Atlanta. I'll even treat you for free."

Back in the United States, I was given two lots of antibiotics. The first didn't work, so I was put on a second, experimental one. The worm never seemed to make an appearance after that dose, and I was grateful. Even then I was aware that I was rapidly working my way through my nine-life limit.

It was now two weeks after the bus crash. Once I was freed from my various tubes, I lived on small doses of watermelon, pineapple, and banana. It seemed no less than a miracle that my intestines were slowly beginning to work again. I was finally out of critical condition but not yet ready to fly. I began to get nervous about the caliber of health care I was receiving, and I wanted to get home as soon as possible. Although my doctor was extremely competent, having just one surgeon perform all the different operations I required—on my arm, my heart, and my lungs—seemed less than ideal. I was getting a number of X-rays every day too, but always without a radiation protection shield. I worried about blood transfusions and AIDS. When we saw a mouse run into my brother's shoe, he made me laugh so hard I had to get my abdominal sutures tightened, but it was the last straw. We had to do something. Andrew maxed out five credit cards and arranged for the twenty-five thousand dollars to fly me back to the States with a paramedic. But it would be another week before I could leave.

Shortly after Andrew arrived, Joe and Jerry had returned to their homes in northern Thailand. Even Roel and Meia had gone back to Holland to mend. I missed them. I felt they were the last link to what I'd been through on that terrible day. Now Andrew needed to go home too—we both knew he had to get back to his family, especially his newborn daughter. His departure was tough on me. I knew what it was to feel like you were never going to see someone again, and I fought the urge to grab him in a hug and not let him leave.

CHAPTER 8

During my time in the hospital in Thailand I received hundreds of well-wishing e-mails and prayers from friends all over the world—all intent on letting me know that I was not alone. It amazed me how quickly the news of my accident had spread. The nurses said that no patient had ever received so many calls; as soon as they heard someone speaking English, the line was put through to me, no matter what time of day or night. Once, thinking it would cheer me up, the nurse even held the phone up to my ear while I was in the middle of painful surgery.

"Hey, how are you?" gushed one of my cheery friends, in a rush of upbeat enthusiasm. Once she realized that I was wincing in pain from the twinge of metal fragments being plucked from my flesh, she kept up an admirable attempt at cheerleading me through the procedure.

Buddhist monks, including the Dalai Lama, were told of my
tenuous condition, and they began doing around-the-clock pujas,
or rituals, for my well-being. During my years living in Nepal, I had
befriended many Tibetans who were living there as refugees. After
the 1959 Tibetan uprising against the Chinese, more than 130,000
Tibetans followed their spiritual and political leader, the Dalai
Lama, into exile and built fifty-seven refugee settlements spread
throughout the neighboring countries of India, Nepal, and Bhutan.
I had devoted years to documenting their lives in photographs.

While lying in bed reading these e-mails, I thought of the
first time I met the Dalai Lama, in 1988. He had heard about
my Tibetan book project, and I was honored to receive an invitation to meet him. I have always so admired him for his enduring
compassion as the leader of the Tibetan people. The survival of
their culture has relied greatly on the guidance and support of this
great man, together with the undying faith the Tibetans have in
Buddhism. The Dalai Lama is considered by the Tibetans to be
the fourteenth reincarnation of Chenrezig, the Buddha of Compassion. Discovered in a remote region of Tibet at the age of two,
Tenzin Gyatso was brought to the Potala Palace in Lhasa, where
he spent his isolated childhood years in training as the newly appointed spiritual and political leader of his country. Although the
Dalai Lama has worked tirelessly in an attempt to preserve what
is left of his culture, time and time again he has stated his desire
to become "just a simple Buddhist monk" and to remove himself
from politics entirely.

When I first met him I was nervous, but he had a way of immediately setting me at ease. He was genuinely interested and concerned with how his people were doing while living in these scattered pocket communities, especially from the perspective of the new generation being raised without a country. His focus was so intense that he made me feel like I was the most important person in the room, and that I was the first to be asking questions that I'm sure he had been asked hundreds of times before.

His now-famous good humor and belly laugh constantly permeated the conversation. As I followed the Dalai Lama into the lushness of his garden, it was a struggle for him to maintain a serious face long enough for me to take a picture; he kept breaking into gales of contagious giggles. We had a full afternoon during that first meeting, and he presented me with a *katag* (an honorific white silk scarf), a Tibetan name (Tenzin Yeshe, Ocean of Wisdom), and an old Tibetan coin. I felt like a child leaving a birthday party, joyful and in awe of my treasures and my new friend.

After that first meeting, I proudly sent photos of the Dalai Lama and me to my parents. Before he won the Nobel Peace Prize, most people, including my family, didn't know who he was or even where Tibet was located. All my parents knew was that I hadn't been back home for years, and now here was a picture of me being embraced by an elderly Asian man in monk's robes, with a shaved head, holding a *mala*, a string of prayer beads. My mother took one look at the photo and called my father in a panic,

"Oh my God, Frank, she's joined a cult. Go over there and get her."

Amazingly, my father and brother actually showed up in Nepal to "rescue" me. I welcomed the opportunity to show them where I lived and the life I'd carved out for myself. Dad loved it, snapping pictures of everything; Andrew, on the other hand, was shocked by the cows and filth crowding the streets of Kathmandu. I didn't even notice such things anymore.

After a few days, I brought them to meet a Tibetan refugee family with whom I'd become very close. Thupten, the father, is a *thangka* painter, an ancient art form in which deities are painted for visualization in Tibetan Buddhist meditation practice. His twin sons are monks, and one has been recognized as a high-reincarnated lama. They also have a younger sister, Domze, and I was lucky to be able to offer financial support to help send her to school. One day I took her to town on the back of my bicycle. She was so excited as we bought her first school uniform and two new pairs of shoes: one for everyday use, the other for special occasions such as the Dalai Lama's birthday. I had asked my dad to bring my old dolls from the attic at home. The next day, when we came to visit them, Barbie and all the other dolls were reverently lined up on the altar. Thupten was worried the children would ruin them.

I told my dad about the Tibetan community in Dharamsala, India. The initial influx of so many Tibetans had raised concern for the welfare of the young children, especially the orphans. The Dalai Lama was quick to take the initiative, and in 1960 created the Tibetan Children's Village, headed by his younger sister, Mrs. Jetsun Pema. The main school and orphanage is based in Dharamsala, and the dorms currently house more than twelve hundred students, although branch schools for three thousand other children are found in many of the settlements in Nepal and India.

Except for monastic purposes, schools were not a common institution in Tibet. In an attempt to marry the old world with the new, Tibetan children in exile are now taught a variety of classes, including their host language, Hindi or Nepali; English; and their native Tibetan. These children were the first in Tibet's history to see maps of the world and hear of the existence of other nations. There are still daily newcomers to the Tibetan Children's Village. Even today parents sneak over the Tibetan border to leave their children so they will receive a Tibetan education.

On one of my visits to Dharamsala I photographed a wave of newly arrived refugee children, some as young as five years old. Each of them had trudged for months over the Himalayan mountain range in the snow, under their own steam, since none of the adults was strong enough to carry them. I was so touched by their plight that I ended up leaving all my clothes and money at the center. I arrived in San Francisco without cab fare or even enough for phone call. I had to call a friend collect to pick me up. Maybe it's not the best idea to get that emotionally involved, but sometimes you can't help yourself.

*   *   *

I figured a short trip to Tibet, introducing them to these benevolent people I had grown to love, was the best way to reassure my family and help them understand my attraction to this culture. I was busy herding our things through the X-ray and chatting in Nepalese with a monk who was bringing a gold Buddha statue to his teacher's monastery in Tibet, when my father looked at me with unexpected awe in his eyes. "I would never be bold enough to go to these places alone," he told me. "I can't believe you're my daughter."

The 1988 trip into Tibet with my dad and brother was one of my first to that country. I have since returned nearly every year for the last two decades. During those first years, Lhasa still held much of the enchantment I had envisioned as a child.

One of my favorite places was the Potala Palace, especially the bedroom of the young Dalai Lama. I imagined him on the night of March 10, 1959, when he had to suddenly flee the familiar world he knew. I especially liked to look out his window. He'd once told me a story of peering through his telescope at the children skating on a pond below, a pond that no longer exists. He told me that as a child he had often felt excruciatingly isolated in the confines of the palace. Besides his brother and tutors, he had no playmates. Once, I saw him walking back into his heavily guarded home in Dharamsala, the metal gate slamming behind him. I asked if he still felt secluded. No, he said, he now had plenty of friends that he knew cared about him. "Besides, I'm a monk!" he added with a laugh.

Now, even his image is banned in Tibet. Once, a Tibetan friend showed me a picture of Mao hanging on the family altar. When she flipped it over, on the other side was a hidden picture of the Dalai Lama.

At the time of that visit with my family, there were only dirt roads surrounding the Potala Palace and leading to the Barkhor, the pulse of Lhasa. Pilgrims flocked to this pilgrimage site from all over Tibet to visit the Jokhang Temple that houses the magnificent gilded Jowo Shakyamuni, the most revered Buddhist statue in Tibet.

Pilgrims circumambulated the Jokhang, surrounded by commerce on one side, religion on the other. Merchants at heart, the Tibetans sold their wares at tables set up all around the impressive temple. Rich yellow yak butter was for sale in giant animal bladders; full flanks of raw meat hung in stalls, freshly killed by members of the small Muslim community. Many years ago, a few Islamic traders passing through had intermarried with Tibetans and settled in Lhasa. Although many of these Tibetan Muslims, who follow the Dalai Lama politically but Mohammed spiritually, were also run out by the Chinese and now live in Srinagar, there are a still a few practicing mosques in the country.

Walking around the Barkhor, Dad bought enough souvenirs to re-create the marketplace in his own home. Back then, there was a treasure trove of goods available: old turquoise-encrusted silver pouches containing flakes of flint wrapped in cotton, for the nomads to start their fires; leather and silver sewing kits encasing large handcrafted steel needles; yak-skin purses adorned with coral and turquoise; and, one of my favorites, *gao*, amulets containing pictures of lamas, and tufts of their hair, teeth, and protection cords. Religious items were for sale everywhere: Buddha statues, yak-bone mala prayer beads, bells and thunderbolt *vajras* used in meditation practice, drinking cups made of human skulls. Old men beckoned us to their back kitchens to show off ornate thangkas with swirling deities and demons. Many had been preserved from the destroyed monasteries and were blackened by years of smoke from yak-butter lamps.

Every day at the Jokhang there was a heavy presence of armed military guards and cameras watched every move. This is where monks and nuns often started the Free Tibet demonstrations, and no more than three people were allowed to stand together as a group. Even so, the indomitable spirit of the Tibetan people is hard to quench. Tall Khampa nomads swaggered about with long red-tasseled braids thrown casually around their heads, fur pelts draped over their shoulders, and long, ornate knives hung from their belts. These were the men who had been feared for years as resistance fighters and bandits—no one messes with the Khampa warriors. Old women, who looked like they were made from the earth itself, spun prayer wheels in a clockwise direction, hoping to bring good karma with each flick of the wrist. Nomadic women from the eastern areas strolled along, a waterfall of amber, coral, and turquoise cascading from headdresses and necklaces. They bargained mercilessly for the giant chunks of colored stones they eyed for sale on the tables. Monks and nuns begged for alms.

The earthy smell of sage permeated the air, wafts of smoke rising from large incense burners. Vendors sold colorful prayer flags that were strung above their tables, sending wishes of peace fluttering to the wind.

On our last afternoon, Dad was tired and went to relax at the hotel while Andrew and I continued to walk around. As we emerged from a small monastery, I suddenly saw a flash of black fur in my periphery. A Tibetan mastiff dog appeared out of nowhere and clamped down on my leg as if it were a much-anticipated pork chop.

I screamed, but this carnivorous animal showed no intention of releasing me. He wouldn't let go until a monk hit him on the head with a plank of wood. My jeans were torn and muddy and stained with the blood seeping through them.

It happened so quickly that I never even had time to register fright. Andrew helped me hobble back to the Holiday Inn. A friend who worked there brought out a medical kit and cleaned me up. He also insisted that rabies shots would be in my best interest.

The "don't tell Dad" mantra didn't work this time—we needed to catch the next flight out to Kathmandu in order to get the injections. Although my dad remained one of my greatest supporters in terms of the work I was doing, I don't think this incident did much to reassure him that I was going to be safe traveling all over the world. And of course, little did he know what was coming.

One day while lying in my Thai hospital bed, I saw on the television that the young Karmapa Lama had escaped into exile to be near the Dalai Lama in India. I had just visited this young lama in central Tibet, and he'd given me the red-silk protection string I was wearing around my neck. In fact, I had often visited him. Each time I left the monastery, I would look back and see him peering down at me from behind his bedroom curtain. When he noticed I was watching him, he would quickly step back, hiding. I thought of the Dalai Lama's childhood years spent in a monastic palace and imagined that the Karmapa was also quite lonely. It had disturbed me how aloof and discontent the Karmapa seemed when I'd visited him this last time. It occurred to me now that he must have been preoccupied with the fact that, like the leader he so revered, he was about to leave his home forever. I touched the string around my neck and silently thanked him for the protection he'd given me. Despite what I'd been through, it could have been worse. I shuddered to think of it, but as I superstitiously stroked my talisman I felt a now familiar wave of gratefulness to be alive. I wished him safety in his new life.

I wondered if I would ever get back to Tibet. I thought about the trip to Mount Kailash in western Tibet I had been planning with some friends when I was in Kathmandu. For years I'd wanted to make the pilgrimage to this holy mountain the Tibetans consider the center of the universe. I looked at my now-useless legs and realized that there was a good chance I would never fulfill this lifelong dream.

Now alone and trapped in my own body, there was little else to do but think. Before he left, Joe had come into my room and, while sitting on the edge of my bed, told me about a conversation he'd had with an American girl he had met while traveling on his way there. Ironically, she had tried to buy a ticket for the same bus that I was on to Vang Vieng and was angry because she had just missed it by moments. She had to wait for the next one, three hours later, and had griped the whole way. Then she came across our demolished bus. When she saw it she burst into tears.

I too had missed the bus I had intended to be on. And the next one had sent me on a whole different path. Yet I had lived while others died. The question of why started to plague me. I didn't believe that life was a series of meaningless random coincidences. Did this crash signify something I was yet to understand?

CHAPTER 9

The third floor of the hospital housed a maternity ward, and every day I asked to be wheeled in front of the rows of bassinets on the way back to my room. Having had so many surgeries, I was greatly comforted watching the rows of precious newborn babies. They were a confirmation of life. They were so small and utterly reliant on others, a vulnerability to which I thoroughly related. There was another thing we shared: I was alive. I felt as though I had been reborn.

Looking through the window at those babies, I thought back to an assignment I had taken for Save the Children a few years before, documenting the basic health-care facilities in a remote region of Nepal. As if to drive the point home, just as I was leaving the area my official-looking car was flagged down by a man whose wife was giving birth by the side of the road. I tried to indicate that my black case was a camera bag and that I was not a doctor. Nevertheless, the driver and I loaded them into our vehicle and drove to the nearest hospital, which was over an hour away. I didn't know anything about delivering babies, but when I saw the arm coming out first, I knew it wasn't a good sign. I can't even find my own pulse in an aerobics class, but I pretended to know what was going on, and it seemed to calm the writhing woman. Once we got to the hospital, we were told that the baby had died, although we had managed to save the mother. Working in such dirt-poor countries was a reminder that life is such a fragile thread, and that the simple fact of where you are born can determine how you will die.

That incident, and many others, made me realize yet again that I was young and an idealist. Against the evidence, I still thought I could help the world with my photos. But when so often faced with these extremes of the human condition I began to question my abilities. While on an assignment in India, a visit to Mother Teresa's orphanage in Calcutta gave me the opportunity to step out from behind the lens of my camera. I was inspired by a quote by Yousuf Karsh, one of the most famous and accomplished portrait photographers of all time. "To make enduring photographs, it is far more important to know about the inner workings of the human mind and soul, for the heart and mind are the true soul of the camera." I needed to physically touch humanity.

The children at the orphanage were doe-eyed beauties in desperate need of love and attention, much like the other children

I had been photographing throughout Asia. Though they were committed to the children's well-being, the nurses betrayed the frustration of the task at hand as they pinched the children's noses while trying to shove food into their mouths and encourage them to eat. One infant I was given to hold was so small I was able to cup him in the palm of my hand. His brown wrinkled skin sagged around his tiny malnourished ankles. Another baby giggled uncontrollably as I threw him into the air. "Hold that beautiful smile, you," I thought.

On Easter Sunday, Mother Teresa came to visit the orphanage and attend Mass. During the service she said something that really resonated with me. "In this life we cannot do great things. We can only do small things with great love." It was hard to believe that this small, shrunken woman from Albania, her face full of wrinkles, had become such a prominent symbol of all that is good in the world. After the service she gave me a blessing and a small silver medallion of the Virgin Mary to wear around my neck. With a knowing smile she encouraged me to visit her home for the destitute and dying.

The next day I hired a rickshaw to take me across town. Dripping with sweat, the rail-thin rickshaw driver dropped me in front of an unpretentious building next to a bathing ghat. Working my way around through the crowd, I stopped at the Kali Temple, where women were praying and tying stone offerings to a cactus tree covered with red china roses.

"This is a fertility tree," a woman in a bright yellow sari said to me. "We come to pray here when we have trouble giving birth." Ironically, as if exemplifying the cycle of life, this was right next to Mother Teresa's Home for the Destitute and Dying in Kalighat, where people would come to spend their last days dying with dignity.

The scene there was intense, humanity at its rawest. The street was lined with the sick and elderly; once inside, I nearly gagged from the strong smell of antiseptic. I was immediately greeted with the sight of a nun carving the dead flesh away from a leper's foot. Another nun, dressed in flowing white robes with blue trim, guided me to the women's area in the back of the building. Half-naked women with shaved heads ran from the staff and volunteers who tried to bathe them, while other patients rocked back and forth on the beds, mumbling incoherently. One woman, her robe open, exposed the fat flesh and bone gaping from an exposed wound on her backside. I felt ashamed by my recoil.

We continued through the room and into the men's area. Again, the smell of antiseptic and infection was overpowering. Men stared at me intently from rows of green cots. Some were hacking, tuberculous; others vomited. There was one more bed to pass before I would be free to head back out the door and into the chaos and sunshine. In the corner, a gray-haired old man, who introduced himself as Sean from Ireland, was trying to feed a much younger Indian man lying on the cot. Sean introduced his ward he had nicknamed Bola, or "strong one." "He's gotten this far," Sean explained.

Bola heard his name and craned his closely shaved head to look at me from the pillow. His eyes were soulful yet imprisoned in his body, which was now flat as a Frisbee from years of lying on a bed. His matchstick bones were twisted and misshapen.

"He seems taken with you," said Sean. "Why don't you try to feed him?"

This was more than I had bargained for. I was, after all, only touring the place, only visiting. I wanted to cuddle children, not confront illness and death like this. Then I remembered that this was what my pilgrimage was actually about: human connection without a camera. So I scooped up a spoonful of the gray gruel, gobs of which were already dribbling from the sides of Bola's mouth, and tried to work it through his partially opened lips. Surprisingly, he managed to keep it down. Then another and another. Sean was amazed.

"We've been trying to feed him for days, and this is the first time he's actually been eating," said Sean incredulously. "He thinks you're an angel."

Sure enough, Bola hadn't stopped staring at me since I began feeding him.

"Will you please come back tomorrow? No one else has been able to get any food into him. We've been afraid he'll die of starvation," Sean said.

I returned every day for the next month. Each morning I made my way through the markets in search of the ripest oranges to squeeze to make juice for Bola. I found bananas, which I mashed to a pulp. I bought Cadbury chocolate bars, the Indian kind, made with wax so they wouldn't melt in the heat. I crushed them down to a fine powder and fed them to Bola when the nurses weren't looking. The treats I brought became our secret. Unable to speak, the love pouring from his eyes said all I needed to know. I wondered about the people in his life who had loved him enough to take care of him this long in such a drastically poor country and then brought him here to die. No one seemed to know anything about his past. He had been left at the doorstep like so many others.

One day Sean asked me to help him bathe a little boy who was in the bed next to Bola. We had named him Toro, "small one." I had tried to feed him, but it had been no use. His skin was peeling away from malnutrition, and he had a hacking, bloody cough from tuberculosis. He was so ill that layers of his skin came away as Sean and I pulled off the bandages. My heart broke as I held his bony body in my arms, trying to absorb his pain. With barely the strength to wince, he put his head on my lap and whimpered.

"Poor thing, he just wants a mum to hold him," said Sean. I stayed late with him, praying for him to die. But his will was so strong, he held on, as if relishing those last minutes in my arms. Eventually, I heard the rattle of death gurgling in his small chest. His eyes gave me a last look before they rolled back into his head and I felt his body go limp.

"What an honor," said Sean. "He chose you to help him die." I was overwhelmed with sadness. I frantically looked around for a nurse, but they were all too busy to deal with what was, sadly, a common occurrence. I thought about Sean's words: this was my responsibility, and mine alone. I wrapped Toro's small body in the still-warm sheet, using a safety pin from my camera bag to close it up. Sean helped me carry him the short distance down the road to the Ganges River. We said a short prayer and dropped the body into the water.

We walked back to the home and made our way to the roof. I looked down at the confusion below us. There was a continuous line of people waiting for a bed inside. It seemed never ending: vacancy by death only.

"I just don't get it," I whispered.

Sean put his arm around me. "You know, my wife died ten years ago. She was the sweetest woman in the world and loved me immensely, but I took her for granted. I was working as a very successful architect in Dublin. I was a philanderer and it hurt my wife greatly. One day she came home and told me that she had been diagnosed with cancer. Ironically, I had to have a triple bypass at the same time, and we spent four months in the hospital together. We grew so close during that period, and it wasn't until then that I really appreciated her. She died the day I left the hospital. After her death I gave up my job and came here to work at Mother Teresa's full time, hoping to redeem myself. I've been here for five years. I still don't have any answers. In my room I have statues of Buddha, Ganesha, and Christ. Who knows what happens to us when we die, but I want to be sure to have my bases covered," he said with a chuckle. "All I know is that one person can't save the world. But if you have touched just a single person then that's something worth living for."

"I guess I had never looked at that way before," I said. "I always thought about the bigger picture."

"Do you know the starfish story?" Sean asked. I shook my head. He told me about a woman who was walking down a beach covered in starfish. As she walked, she saw a man carefully picking up starfish one at a time and gently placing them back into the ocean.

"Are you crazy?" the woman had asked. "What difference is that ever going to make, with these hundreds of starfish?"

He smiled and answered, "It made a difference to that one."

I had to return to my work in Nepal, but I was always going back and forth to India and returned to Calcutta a year later. Bola's bed was empty. No one there even remembered him.

But I do.

Now I was looking at rows of cherubic babies in Thailand, and thoughts of sweet Bola and Toro came to my mind. I would always be inspired by their strength at facing death and their ability to shine with love even in their final days. As for me, I was not out of the woods yet, but for the first time I felt sure that I would see my family again. Through the surges of pain, a feeling of elation was creeping in. It was good to keep repeating those three words: "I am alive." In the safe cocoon of the hospital, I contemplated the life before me, the death behind me, and again the question nagged: Why did I survive while others didn't?

As I slowly gained my strength, Dr. Bunsom came to visit me in my room one afternoon. "I know you're anxious about leaving," he told me. "I think you may finally be strong enough to be transported to a hospital in San Francisco. I'm concerned about your fragile lungs holding up on the flight, but we've arranged to have a paramedic fly with you in case you need a tracheotomy." Knowing my affinity for Asia and that it looked like it would be a very long time before I would be back again, if ever, he asked, "Is there anything you would like to do before you leave?"

I told him that I would like to go to a temple, and I was surprised when he actually arranged for an ambulance to take me to Wat Pa Ban Tat, a monastery famous for visits from the Thai princess Maha Chakri Sirindhorn. It was my first outing, about a forty-five-minute ride stretched out in the back of the ambulance. Once we arrived, I awkwardly managed to make my way to the altar with the use of canes and the help of two paramedics who carried me partway. My senses felt heightened, and the world now seemed loud and full of sharp objects. I missed the safety of my room, my soft bed. But I knew I couldn't stay there forever. I had to find the strength to move back into the world. The giant gold-leafed Buddha smiled down on us as Thai families made their offerings of gigantic bowls of fresh fruit. Each person knelt before the giant statue, a sweet smelling incense stick wafting from between their squeezed palms.

I offered a prayer of gratitude for my survival. I murmured my appreciation for all those strangers, some of whom had risked their lives, and what they had done to help me endure this ordeal: the young man who sewed up my arm and the villagers who tended to me; Alan, who had driven me out of there; the men from the American embassy who met me and were instrumental in opening the Thai-Lao Friendship Bridge; Dr. Bunsom, for all the lifesaving surgeries, and his attentive staff; my brother; and the loyal tribe of friends and family who continued to support me.

As I sat meditating, trying to take in all that had happened, a young man invited me to have tea with the head monk and some of his students. Sitting with the monks, I reflected on all that had happened to me. I took great comfort in their calming presence. With the help of a student translator, I told them about the accident and those last moments of pure blissful awareness as I realized life as I knew it was seeping away from me. "I felt that I had been truly touched by the hand of a higher power. In that small, fleeting moment of enlightenment I felt seamlessly connected to a part of something organically bigger than ourselves. It's like I've discovered a state of grace, an inner freedom, that I can't ever again believe that we are separate beings on individual paths. I know we're all here with a purpose, but I can't help but feel I lived for a reason. I'm just not sure what that reason is."

The head monk nodded in understanding as he handed me a steaming cup of tea. "Ah, a bodhisattva." He smiled. "And now you have the opportunity to share this experience with others, to bring an open heart of compassion and understanding to a world that is in such desperate need of it."

"During my time in the hospital, I thought a lot about our will to live," I told him. "It amazes me how innately we want to be here." I know that deep down I played a conscious part in my initial survival, but really it is quite remarkable how tenacious our bodies are, and even after the pain of such devastating injuries has set in, how much we endure the healing in order to continue on with our lives. "I just don't know what that means for me now," I continued. I took a deep breath while placing my empty teacup onto the table next to me.

The monk shook his head in a sympathetic gesture as he offered me his parting words. "You must move forward from this experience," he told me, "and not dwell on looking back." He motioned for the translator to give me some meditation books he had written.

Living among the compassionate Buddhist cultures of Asia had brought undeniable insight and wisdom to my life. The people I'd encountered helped me realize that spirituality isn't just about chanting prayers and ritual. It's a way, embedded in our consciousness, we choose to live our lives. I believe that our actions today create our future experiences: we get what we give. If we move through the world with love, we will receive it in return. If we move through the world with anger and bitterness, that is what will come back at us. I had long been attracted to the idea of karma. If we don't learn from our mistakes, we are doomed to repeat them over and over until we get it right. I felt that this accident happened for a reason, and as with every challenge, there was a lesson for me to learn from it.

Was I meant to have some great spiritual awakening from this close brush with death? The reality was sinking in. Yes, I was happy to be alive, but I was now faced with profound challenges. What would my new life be like, and, even more important, who was this invalid person I had now become?

PART II

a hard road back

Life is full of suffering—and overcoming it.
                                    —HELEN KELLER

CHAPTER 10

It was time to go home.

I was accompanied on the flight from Thailand back to the United States by a young Australian paramedic. While I was being loaded onto the plane, I noticed that he quite happily accepted the complimentary glass of champagne offered by the flight attendant.

I, on the other hand, lay on my back, ensconced in pillows. The attendants did their best to make me comfortable, but it was probably a good thing that I was heavily sedated for the long trip. Once we were airborne the drugs began to kick in. The mix of Percocet and morphine made me woozy but talkative.

"I lived in Australia for a couple of years," I told the champagne drinker. "I photographed my way around the country, living out my cowgirl dreams while on a cattle ranch in the dusty, isolated outback; working on a dive boat in the Great Barrier Reef; and living in Sydney. Until I'd run out of money and overstayed my visa, that is."

As I told my story, he barely looked up from his magazine. The cocktails cart had come by, and he'd moved on to white wine with his dinner. So I kept talking, not caring if he listened or not.

"Travel. Meet people," the ad in the Sydney newspaper had read. "Barmaid needed in Port Hedland, Western Australia."

I'd never served drinks before in my life, but "How hard can it be?" I'd thought. When the owner of the Pier Hotel told me he was paying two hundred Australian dollars a week under the table with room and board, it seemed like a good deal. He informed me that the last girl had left in tears; I foolishly neglected to ask why. He was desperate, which is why he was willing to hire me sight unseen.

"What's your name?" he asked. I quickly remembered to give him an alias, "Ali Weston."

The bar looked like something out of *Crocodile Dundee*. After a grueling twenty-four-hour bus ride from Perth, I finally reached the place, but my exhaustion evaporated as I worked my way through the raucous crowd. Dreadlocked Aboriginals and dust-covered men wearing filthy denim shorts and nursing beers catcalled at me, making me wish I was wearing a suit of armor rather than a sundress. Hoisting my backpack on my shoulder and giving them my best don't-screw-with-me look, I finally made it to the bar. The customers were actually beating their palms on the countertops as I sidled up to the counter.

I was greeted by the owner who was slobbering on his burned-out stub of a cigar. "You can pour beer, right?"

"Of course," I told him. Okay, so only into my own mouth, but I didn't need to tell him that. There was a tap on my shoulder, and I turned around to see the man next to me promptly take a bite from his beer mug. As he chewed on the glass with a smile, I could see from his jagged teeth that there had been many previous attempts at perfecting this party trick. I was immediately intrigued by the challenge of becoming immersed in this subculture. "Huh," I thought, "I'm going to have to stay here for a while."

Port Hedland was an ugly, one-main-street mining town. Huge piles of salt lined the roadside, waiting to be loaded onto barges. Red dust coated everything, including the people. It was home to mostly Aboriginals, but workers arrived by ship from all over the world to work here as miners, electricians, and as construction workers. The main form of entertainment—well, the only form of entertainment—was drinking.

I was put to work immediately. The first beer I poured was for a crusty old man sitting at the end of the bar. As I handed it to him, a fist came out of nowhere knocking his head to the side like in a *Popeye* cartoon. "FIIIIIIGHT!" wailed a war call from somewhere in the back of the crowd. Kay, who at twenty years old was only slightly younger than me, was a tough "professional barmaid," and knew the drill, dragging me into the walk-in cooler. As we sat on a keg of beer freezing our butts off, she explained that the fights, mostly between the Aboriginals and whites, were a nightly ritual. Like a bomb shelter, this was the safest place to hide out while the combatants proceeded to trash the bar and beat each other to a bloody pulp until the cops arrived.

Subsequent nights were just as eventful. The heavyset, fish-eyed owner, Henry, and his son, Mike, thrived on either verbally abusing me or leaving me to my own devices to survive the crowd each night. They seemed determined to see me break, which only made me more resolved to stay. Fortunately, I had support from the "permanent dwellers," the regulars who drank there every day. "Ali, you keep pouring that beer, and we'll keep drinking it," they encouraged. My newfound friends didn't care if the beer sloshed on the counter and was foamy. Mike, the son, did nothing except, with a perpetual scowl on his face, constantly spray the bar counter with toxic insect repellent, getting it in people's food, their faces. "The flies might be annoying," I told him, "but that's no reason to poison the customers."

In the States, bartenders are supposed to feel some responsibility for their client's alcohol consumption, but in that part of Australia the house rule was to serve as long as the customer could keep coughing up money for his drinks. This often meant serving people until they passed out—or threw up. Whenever that happened, the drill was to take away the beer, replace it with a glass of water (in case the police came and caught us serving drunks), and always to make sure to collect on the tab. One guy drank until he spewed all over the bar, at which point he passed out on the floor. After a few minutes of slumber, he managed to clamber back up, yelling, "I'm hungry!" which had us all in stitches—except for the guy with vomit on his shoes, who proceeded to give him a judo chop in the face. Down for the count he went once again.

I've been told the Pier Hotel is in the *Guinness Book of Records* for being the most dangerous pub in the world. I'm not sure that's true, but it certainly wouldn't surprise me. Working there was like being a voyeur on another planet.

Weeks went by. There were fights every night. Not only had all the pool cues been snapped in half, rendering the pool table useless, but we had now lost all the disco equipment to barroom brawls. Despite the danger, I soon gained enough confidence to stand my ground. Sure, we had to duck as beer bottles went whizzing past our heads, breaking into pieces against the steel refrigerators behind us, but the fistfights no longer perturbed me as they once did. The walls were full of holes people had punched out of anger and frustration, or just for practice until they got to the real thing. I was thankful for the handwritten sign scribbled in pencil above the door: "Please don't hit the bar staff."

That said, I did manage to have a romantic reprieve from the insanity. A fair-haired New Zealander named Ross was working in the town as an electrician, and though he was a drunk, he was a jovial one. I found having a strapping bodyguard-boyfriend at the bar not necessarily a bad thing.

Sadly, Ross didn't fare well with Hermann. Hermann the German seemed to be just another harmless drunkard as he planted himself at the end of the bar and asked for a beer. But the heat and isolation of life in Port Hedland—in addition to the drinking—could turn anyone's brain into a gooey substance (a state the Aussies affectionately described as "gone tropo").

"You're too beautiful to be hidden away here in this bar in the middle of nowhere," Herman told me as I placed his drink in front of him.

"Don't worry," I told him, "I don't plan to be here forever."

"Oh, you say that now, young lady. I want to take you away from all this. Marry me." He stood up unsteadily, waving his arm with a flourish for emphasis. I rolled my eyes and walked away. I figured I must have been proposed to over a beer glass about a half-dozen times a day. But Hermann was different—he was persistent. He returned that afternoon with a handwritten résumé explaining why he would be a good husband. To my eyes he still looked like a loony old goat, so I turned him down. Then the poems and love stories started coming. His constant bellowing of his eternal affections from the bar stool was starting to embarrass and, quite frankly, scare me. This seemed to be the new form of evening entertainment—except that I had to put up with it all night. Every day. For a week.

One day, the police arrived. Not an unusual occurrence around those parts, but this time they made a beeline for me. Apparently, the night before they had arrested Hermann for disturbing the peace, but he had escaped from jail. He had since been recaptured

and they had a summons, under my assumed name, for me to tes-
tify in court that he had been stalking me. For someone who was
working in the country illegally and trying to keep a low profile, I
was certainly getting a lot of attention.

Ross came with me to court; Hermann kept looking at Ross,
threatening to fight him. That was not good. While we were waiting, I watched a long line of Aboriginals I recognized from the bar
show up for various court appearances. Then it was Hermann's
turn. He plead guilty.

"This is quite a serious offense, escaping from prison," the
judge scolded him. "Would you like to tell the courtroom why
you did this, Hermann?"

Whirling around the courtroom, he pointed his finger directly
at me.

"Because of her!" he yelled. "I love her! I want to marry her
and take her away from all this!"

The whole courtroom, which because Hermann had escaped,
included the entire local police force, burst into hysterical laughter. I was mortified.

"I understand," said the judge. "We've all fallen in love with
pretty young barmaids before. But still, you have to leave her
alone," he warned. The judge decided to let Hermann off on
probation.

Big mistake.

Kay and I shared a bedroom above the bar. Needless to say,
Hermann pounded on our bedroom door during the day and con-

tinued clamoring over me in the bar in the evening. I was furious with Henry for not banning him. One night, after yet another round of declarations of his love, Henry had had enough, and backhanded Hermann right across the face. "And I should do the same to you for leading him on," he yelled.

If I hadn't guessed before, now it was clear: Henry was psychotic. I quit.

A group of us went to the bar next door for drinks, to let off steam, but Hermann followed us and tried to kill Ross with a hammer. Ross, who was the most passive person you could imagine, simply floored Hermann with a red plastic chair. After yet more assaults on my bedroom door with the hammer, Hermann was finally removed and committed to the sanatorium. The other guys from the bar presented me with a wad of cash they'd taken up as a collection, enough to get me the hell out of this place.

After seven weeks of madness, I was more than ready to move on. Shortly after I left Australia, the Pier Hotel closed down.

The paramedic was now wrapping up his meal with a glass of port. His glassy eyes blinked at the end of my story.

"Oh, and by the way," I said, "under no circumstances are you performing a tracheotomy on me if I need one." And with that, I settled back into watching the blood-curdling *Blair Witch Project*, which had been looping over and over on my personal DVD player. Not a good choice, I quickly realized, when high on morphine.

CHAPTER 11

*A*nd then I was back in the States.

The transition was an abrupt one, to say the least. In Asia, Dr. Bunsom had arranged for an ambulance to take me to visit a monastery. Back in the United States, my injuries apparently didn't even warrant an ambulance ride from the airport. Dana and Carole picked us up to transport me directly to the hospital in San Francisco. The woman from the airlines who was pushing me in a wheelchair waited while my friends gingerly, but awkwardly, helped me into the car. I was touched by the woman's concern until she announced that she was waiting for a tip.

"Wow, I already gave her a ten," Dana said.

Once we were at the hospital, the Australian paramedic simply parked me in the emergency ward, along with my voluminous medical charts, all of which were written in Thai. We never saw him again. I was elated to be under American care and felt a wave of relief as soon as the ER doctor walked through the door. After forcing myself to be strong for nearly three weeks, I finally allowed myself to feel vulnerable and to be cared for. I was home.

The first thing the doctors wanted to do was cut off the Buddhist protection string the Karmapa Lama had given me in Tibet. I had worn it around my neck for all my surgeries, and I was adamant about keeping it on—it had gotten me this far. The doctors in San Francisco, who after assessing my injuries started calling me "the miracle kid," didn't have a better theory and agreed to let me keep wearing it.

"We don't know if we could have saved you even if you'd come directly to our emergency room after such a debilitating accident," Dr. Wong, the tall attending physician told me while leaning over my bed.

"Yeah, Princess Diana died of one of the same internal injuries—a herniated heart—and she'd been minutes from a Paris hospital," a handsome male nurse with dreadlocks said as he moved me onto a gurney to be wheeled to the radiation department. I shuddered as I remembered the young man in Laos with the same hair—and with a metal rod going through his cheek.

Because my Thai-speaking paramedic was presumably now touring the San Francisco wine country, no one could read my chart. It would be weeks before we could get it translated. I felt a bit like a baby left on a doorstep. The doctors had to x-ray and image every body part and start from scratch. With my broken bones, it was unbearable to lie on the hard surfaces for long enough to get MRIs and CT scans. With the more advanced digital imaging in this country the doctors were able to pinpoint a pelvic fracture and other breaks that couldn't be seen clearly through ordinary X-rays in Thailand. An image of my arm showed that it was still peppered with debris, but at least it appeared that I had all my internal organs. Hearing the results, I again realized how lucky I was.

The doctor pointed out that this was the second time I'd broken my tailbone. He didn't need to remind me—I had taken a hard fall on it the previous year while snowboarding. I don't know how many times one can break a coccyx, but I made a promise to myself to stow my Rollerblades in the back of my closet for good.

The nurse spent the day with me, taking my blood, making me drink vile barium solution, and wheeling me around the hospital for various tests.

By evening I was exhausted. The flight had been arduous, and I'd since seen a barrage of doctors. Notes were made, prescriptions were written, and further surgeries were scheduled. But there was a flu epidemic and not only was nearly every bed in the hospital filled but the doctors were concerned that with my compromised lungs I was susceptible to infection.

I was released and sent back to my apartment.

After a fitful night in my own bed, I had awakened in the early dawn gasping for air. I called my neighbor, Carmine, in a panic. "I can't breathe! Please come over!" I felt like I was suffocating, and

I was terrified. Carmine flew through my door just as my phone started to ring.

"This is Dr. Wong in emergency. I called to see if you're having any trouble breathing. I just looked at your lung X-ray, and you need to get right back in here as soon as possible. It's bad. We shouldn't have let you go." I hung up before he could finish. Carmine drove me to the emergency room as I gripped the dashboard of his car. My lungs felt like a tube from which someone was trying to squeeze the last bit of toothpaste. Something was wrong, terribly wrong.

I had flown sooner than I should have, and my lungs had collapsed and once again filled with fluid. My breathing was shallow and rapid as they raced me into the ER. A lung specialist rushed in, and I grimaced as he inserted a fine tube through my back and into my chest to aspirate my lungs.

"After what you've gone through, I'd think this would hardly faze you," the doctor said as he attempted to wind the tube through my twisted rib cage as gently as he could. But it didn't work that way. The ability to handle such intense pain while under extreme distress must have come from somewhere in my deepest depths. Now I was my old self again—flinching at even the sight of a needle.

"You know," I said to the doctor, while I tried to relax, "I once asked the Dalai Lama in an interview if anything ever made him nervous and tense. You know what he said? Needles. That and meeting religious and world leaders."

"Well, it sounds like you're in good company," the doctor laughed, finally straightening the thin wire protruding from my back. "You're all set now; we've got the lung drain in. You did great. Now let's go see if we can roust up some world leaders for you."

Despite all I'd gone through, I wasn't any more comfortable with the anticipation of physical discomfort. I had survived. I felt like I had acted on an inherent instinct. Dealing with the pain of mending was now going to be the hard part.

"You realize you should be dead," Dr. Roberts, my newly appointed primary care physician, told me as he reviewed my recently translated chart.

"Yeah, I've heard."

"No, I'm serious," he said. "You have to be aware of the extent of your injuries—the sutures inside, the scars outside, the broken bones."

"We're going to try sending you home again," he went on, "but because you live on your own, you'll have to find someone to drive you to the hospital almost daily for doctors' appointments. You'll have to rely completely on friends for at least the next three months and do absolutely nothing but convalesce." My friend Linda had accompanied me to this meeting, and the doctor gave her a hard glance. Her worried eyes peered at me through her dark bangs and she sighed. Amid the triangle of looks, I think we all had the same thought: "Rely totally on others and do nothing but convalesce?"

I was not going to be an easy patient.

My life came to a complete halt. For the first twelve weeks I lay in bed at home in a morphine-induced haze as my bones slowly knitted. I had no idea how restorative sleep could be. I was so doped up I was concerned that I had brain damage. It was difficult to complete sentences and to remember people's names. I used to be a voracious reader. Now books were too challenging, and I found myself flipping through *People* magazine or watching mindless TV, transfixed by VH1 reruns such as "Whatever Happened to John Denver?" I couldn't even feed or bathe myself.

I had traveled the world: sailed on every ocean, stepped on every continent, traversed two thousand miles down the Amazon in a decrepit fishing boat to photograph shamans, trekked to the Everest Base Camps on both the Nepal-Tibet sides and hiked to Machu Picchu. I had always been fiercely independent, and now I was forced to completely depend on others. I despised being weak and needy. But my friends rallied, providing around-the-clock care in my home, always making sure I was fed and well taken care of. At first it was a challenge for me to accept assistance. I was reluctant to ask for anything; I felt like such a burden.

And then a friend pointed out that I had this wonderful support system of people who wanted to do things for me. It gave them joy to help alleviate my suffering. This was an important lesson in accepting help from others. I felt like I had come back for my own funeral just to feel that love. I didn't know that people cared that much. That was the greatest gift of all.

"We brought you soup!" shouted my neighbors as they entered my apartment with their spare key. Carmine cracked open the door to my bedroom with his endearing Japanese partner, Hideo, behind him, balancing a giant bowl of steaming vegetables in his hand.

"It's your favorite restaurant in San Francisco delivering," Hideo said. During the fifteen years of living next door to each other we'd often pooled the contents of our refrigerators. With enviable ease, they'd whip up something delicious for dinner, and as I'm an appalling cook, I'd supply the wine. Their creative, mouthwatering meals was always a much-appreciated welcome-home treat after a long trip. And now, while I was bedridden, they insisted on preparing me healthy food to eat.

"I brought you some roses from the garden," Carmine said, pushing back the familiar black beret that was always balanced sideways on his head.

Potters and painters, Carmine and Hideo were continually involved in creating art or remodeling their apartment. When they got bored decorating their place, they'd set their sights on mine. There were times in the past when I'd walked out of my kitchen to find my whole living room being rearranged. Not that I'd minded. In fact it would never occur to me even to paint my apartment without consulting them first. They were my family, now more so than ever.

The generosity that shone my way was endless. Friends shipped my belongings back from Nepal. Bob handled the endless calls and paperwork for insurance claims. Lynn, who has a house-keeper do her own home, vacuumed. Christi installed a handrail in my bathroom so I could eventually bathe on my own. Dana and Carole visited often and even brought homemade lasagna. Paul set up a small fountain in my room so I could hear the soothing sound of water, and then gently shoved me to the other side of the bed so we could sit watching videos over large bowls of popcorn. Other friends brought lavender oil, vitamin E lotion, and creams to help soothe my angry scars. They shopped, brought movies to watch, drove me to doctors' appointments.

The days melted into each other. That three months was the longest span of time I'd spent at home for as long as I could re-member. My apartment in San Francisco was not a place I saw often; I was constantly on the road. There were no plants, and my last pets had been fish. I returned home from a trip that was longer than anticipated to find that the water had totally evapo-rated, leaving nothing but skeletal remains on the bottom of the fish tank. I still live with the guilt, imagining their last moments gasping for air.

The career of a travel photographer is a rather self-involved lifestyle choice. The profession demands a level of commitment and passion that seems to embed itself in our very being. Even with my worldwide connections, it can sometimes make for a lonely life to commit yourself for weeks, months, even years at a time to becoming part of another culture. We miss our family's birthdays, weddings, and even deaths. Despite this, I am grateful for the great clan of friends I have from all corners of the globe. They seem to accept the fact that I will always be in their lives, even though I am constantly dipping in and out. Given how much I needed friends now, I was glad that was the case. I wouldn't be going anywhere for a while.

I again developed a high threshold of tolerance for pain. As each injury vied for attention, it was impossible to quantify the amount of soreness, but I would say the broken ribs and pelvis were tied for the worst. In fact, one day Dr. Wong called to say he'd broken his pelvis while taking a fall from his bike:

"I had to tell you how much empathy I have for you now. In all my years of treating these broken bones, I had no idea how incredibly severe the pain is."

"And you thought I was just trying to get attention," I laughed.

To avoid putting any excessive pressure on my mending bones I was forced to lie on my back, but no matter how I moved it was impossible to get comfortable. Besides morphine, I was on an array of other opiates, but nothing affected the steady pain, and I was constantly nauseated. Having the morphine and cortisone epidurals administered directly into my spine was difficult to bear, even though the drugs helped the discomfort. I alternated heating pads with ice packs until I was eventually able to have a daily soak in a hot bath with salts. But it would be many years before I could lie on my side again, and even then I received cortisone shots in my hips for the bursitis that had set in.

The nerve damage from my spinal injury made my skin prickle and itch as if I had an extreme sunburn, and I could barely tolerate the feel of even the softest bedsheets against my body. After a few weeks of this, I was desperate for a reprieve.

My mother arranged for a reflexologist to come to the house. For the first visit she massaged only my hands, the one part of my body that hadn't been affected. After so many invasive procedures it was a welcome feeling to be touched in a therapeutic way. "It's important to find even temporary relief," the therapist told me. "The more you live with pain, the more you feel it. When you're immersed in it, the receptors have a heightened awareness. However you can manage it, you have to reset your pain fibers with a few hours of relief. If you don't, you're sending a message to your body that you're willing to put up with this and it becomes chronic." A few hours! I'd be thrilled with five minutes.

Oddly enough, my horoscope for that day, January 30, 2000, was a keeper: "Don't be surprised if you can't move. You've been through a lot, and your psyche needs to recuperate."

At other times, the nerve damage caused me to have no feeling in my arms at all. Test results were inconclusive. My physical therapist would try to stimulate movement in my legs with the use of electrodes and attempt to break up some of the scar-tissue damage with ultrasound treatments, but I wasn't getting my leg strength back. I grew frustrated with the lack of encouragement and support from many of my physicians. Too often, it seemed to me, they delivered a grim prognosis when I would have preferred some hope to come my way. I soon began to realize that the many specialists treating me had little confidence that I would ever walk properly again.

Dr. Jann Johnson, on the other hand, was one of my most compassionate doctors. She had worked as a plastic surgeon in the Bay Area as well as in third world countries, helping children with cleft palates, for which I greatly admired her.

With all the glass and metal fragments still embedded in my arm, it became, as feared, infected a number of times. Every few months, Dr. Johnson would remove debris from what she called the "garbage dump" in my arm. Scars were removed, the skin was resutured, and the healing process began all over again. Occasionally, bits of glass would find their way out on their own, and I would tape them into my journal. On bad days, the pieces would get stuck under my skin, and I'd end up in the hospital with blood poisoning. (I will probably live with this for the rest of my life and must always carry antibiotics with me.)

"We never see jagged scarring such as this," she told me, "because we have safety glass in this country." She gave me no false hope that I'd ever have an attractive torso or arm again, but we both worried that the extent of damage to the skin would ultimately limit my mobility. If I were to resume taking photos, I desperately needed the use of both my arms.

To help heal the wounds on my left arm, I wore a compression-therapy sleeve for just over a year, seven days a week, twenty-three hours a day. I could remove it only for showering. I despised wearing it. This binding garment is the same bandaging that is worn by burn patients, and it is incredibly hot and uncomfortable; but if it worked, it would help maintain the movement in my arm and preserve my muscles. The tight-fitting mesh sleeve would help reduce the tissue damage from the thick keloid scars I had developed, which is unusual for light-skinned people.

I was also treated with intensely painful steroid injections and made to wear unwieldy silicone patches. Dr. Zachary at UCSF began excruciating laser surgeries to break down the "traumatic tattooing," the bits of black gravel and glass still trapped under the skin. Eventually, I would start dermabrasion treatments to try and flatten the scars to further help my mobility. Despite my initial discomfort, I still felt a profound appreciation every time I reached for something. At least I had an arm.

I woke up bathed in sweat and peeked through my blinds. The streets were wet and my neighbors' red SUV sat parked across the street unharmed. I realized that the sound of the car accident that had jarred me awake had been just been another bad dream. I battled these recurring nightmares of crashing vehicles, shattered glass, and strewn bodies nearly every night. As I lay back on my pillows, exhausted, all I really wanted to do was sleep, but ever since the accident it had not come easily. When I did finally drift off, I had terrible dreams.

Everyone had a suggestion for combating my overwhelming insomnia, and I tried them all: warm milk, herbal remedies, hot baths, chamomile tea, wine, but often I found myself simply resorting to prescription drugs. Even they couldn't seem to calm my tension and discomfort. I was so medicated that I would eventually pass out for short periods of time. Sleeping through the night was another matter. There were occasions when I woke up to screams. Alone in the dark, it took some time before I realized they were my own.

While sitting in Dr. Roberts's office during one of my visits, six weeks after arriving back in San Francisco, I opened my notepad. Inside were notes from a tarot reading I'd had in Seattle the previous year. I read the last line as I waited for the results from my chest X-ray: "Watch your lungs, take care of them. Breathe deeply."

My life now revolved around the hospital. I had been tested for AIDS and hepatitis, as the doctors had been worried about tainted blood during my treatment in Thailand. "How ironic would that be," I thought as I flipped through my medical charts that were now as thick as phone books. I'd had my share of illnesses from years of world travels and words jumped from the page: giardia, dysentery, worms, malaria, hepatitis, typhoid, dengue fever while in Asia (health department notified), eyes burned from tear gas in Nepal, coccyx broken while snowboarding. Patient has good friends, Buddhist beliefs, is on Percocet, Vicodin, morphine. Questions when she can go trekking, kayaking, travel.

"Post-traumatic stress?" The question was circled in red atop the myriad pages referring to the accident. I felt almost detached reading this litany, until I remembered—the charts were mine.

"So, how are you?" Dr. Roberts asked as he walked into the room.

"I'm good. Look, I'm finally hobbling around on my own with a cane." I was always keen to show off my progress.

"Okay, cut the bullshit. How are you really doing?" he said. And then he surprised me by sharing his own story. "You know, I'm a cancer survivor myself, and even though my own near-death ordeal can't compare to yours, I know this must be a profound experience for you."

I was shocked. He seemed so young and healthy.

"Well actually, I'm still having a lot of trouble sleeping," I admitted. "Not only am I in constant pain, but my skin is so sensitive and itchy. And these horrific nightmares won't let up. It's always a different variation of the same theme: terrible car accidents with so much blood. What gets me is that they seem so real."

He nodded his head. "Okay, I'm sending you for an evaluation. I also want you to keep up your meditation practice, even if you do it while just lying in bed." He pointed toward the cane. "Try walking meditation in your apartment too." Dr. Roberts spun his chair around toward the computer and set up appointments for me to see a lung specialist, a plastic surgeon, and a psychiatrist.

I grabbed the ugly metal cane that made me feel a hundred years old and started to leave.

"Hey, tough girl."

"Yeah?"

"It's not a sign of weakness to work through some of these

emotions, you know. That was quite a harrowing experience you had."

I half smiled. I had a feeling he knew what he was talking about.

Dr. Roberts was right—I hated to admit anything was wrong with me. But sure enough, a few weeks later I was diagnosed with post-traumatic stress disorder.

To my surprise I actually liked Jennifer, my therapist. She was middle-aged with graying hair, and I found her very approachable. She also displayed a strong spiritual side that appealed to me. For the first time I spoke about my awful nightmares.

"Even though you wanted to panic and be taken care of, you had to pull in all your resources and put it toward your own survival," Jennifer told me. "And now you are so intent on focusing on the physical healing, the emotions are having to take a backseat. Except at night when the demons rear their ugly heads."

"But apart from that, I feel fine," I told her. "In fact, I actually feel this overwhelming euphoria at being alive."

It was true. I was constantly being struck by small but sublime moments of beauty. I could be lost for an hour just watching a patch of sunshine dancing on my kitchen table. I would taste, really taste, the succulent sweetness of green grapes. I sat in my backyard relishing the warmth of the sun and for the first time actually seeing the exuberant colors of the flowers so lovingly tended by Carmine and Hideo. My once huge world had become so small, but there was an advantage to that: there was a time when I had raced past all these things in life, but not anymore.

As my physical healing progressed, I continued to experience intense emotions. Mostly I felt euphoric, reborn, able to appreciate people and experiences more deeply. Each morning as I pulled myself out of bed and placed my feet on the floor, I felt grateful just to be here. Everyday things took on a profundity they hadn't had before. I would be pushing my cart through the supermarket aisles and feel an immense love for the people around me. I would see a bus on the Golden Gate Bridge and secretly wish all the passengers safety. People walking down the beach became recipients of a loving-kindness meditation I had learned, turning my thoughts toward others: "May you be happy, may you be peaceful."

My heart, once so damaged, now felt so centered and my feelings of tenderness ran deep. In my own way I knew I was bestowing blessings on those around me. I felt so connected to a universal power of grace that I wanted to share it. As I focused this positive intention on other people, I liked to believe they were walking away feeling something tangible, and in return supporting someone else. Most often I wished those whom I encountered protection from harm.

The world seemed vibrant and electrified, and I believed the continuation of my life to be one giant postscript. The taste of death became a touchstone, reminding me of what seemed truly important—family, friends, and a desire to give something back to the world through my work. "Open your heart and you'll become a magnet for all you're looking for," I had once read, and I found this to be true. My own heart had expanded to a capacity I hadn't realized it was capable of.

But there were, I eventually admitted, very dark days indeed. I hated to complain to my friends about my latest ailments and surgeries, and I rarely vocalized my struggles even on my most miserable days. Fortunately, my sessions with Jennifer became a good place to vent.

"Here I was young and athletic one day, and the next I feel like I've turned into an aged cripple overnight. I hate coming to this hospital every day," I told her. I didn't know if it was all the trauma to my body, a reaction to the drugs I was on, or the fact that I could see no reprieve from this chronic pain, but there were days I had to admit that I was truly depressed. I was always so tired, I worried if I would ever get my energy back. There were times I didn't know if I could continue being encased in a body that brought me so much unrelenting misery. "The doctors all seem so pessimistic in regards to my recovery," I said, "and no one can give me answers as to when I'll be better. It's the not knowing that brings me into the tunnel of darkness and questioning if this is how I'll be for the rest of my life."

And then Jennifer consoled me with the same sentiments that the monk had shared with me in Thailand. "Even in the darkness all we can do is keep moving forward," she told me.

It wasn't that I wanted to die. But I had tasted the sweet nirvana of death, and I was no longer afraid to go there.

What I couldn't talk about, though, was that I was feeling a little gypped. Lying in that room in Laos I had surrendered to death and transitioned to an incredibly peaceful place, one of profound light and all-encompassing love. My heart had never felt so open. I had dipped more than just a toe over to the other side, and I longed for that place. It soon became clear that I was part of a very small club of people who had experienced this afterlife, and I simply wasn't able to easily open the door back to the life I once knew. I felt isolated, as if I were still separated from the rest of the world, looking from the other side of a steamy window. I've been intimate with other people's deaths, I just never imagined I'd be so close to my own. To be here now was a gift, but I came back for what? More pain and a quagmire of insurance claims? I had gone through so much, but for what purpose?

"My days have become so boring," I said to Jennifer in another session, after being in bed for three tedious months. I told her that I was used to a life of excitement and change. I was the queen of multitasking, always juggling numerous projects. Even as a kid I hated to sleep, I hated the thought of missing something. When I was working, my life was always on the move. I was rarely at home. The first question everyone used to ask me was, "Where are you going to next?"

I hadn't just sampled life—I had inhaled every experience with an unrelenting hunger. I was constantly in motion—I wanted to see everywhere, taste every food, and meet every person I possibly could. I decided long ago that if I were to have regrets they were to be over things I had done, not things I had missed doing. I always felt there was never enough time. I was now looking at the world through the other end of the telescope. And time was all I had.

I had gone somewhere that I couldn't photograph or document. I couldn't even talk about it—there was no vocabulary to describe this place, this feeling. Besides, I desperately wanted to hang on to this very personal and sacred journey, and I felt that to talk about it would diminish the experience.

When I thought back to my old self there would be moments of sadness and yearning for that healthy person. If I considered the future, I often realized that I faced a lot of uncertainty, especially with regard to my physical capabilities. It was during the difficult days when I realized that if I trained my mind to truly be in the present moment, it was almost impossible to be unhappy. No matter how bad it got, there was an internal curiosity about how this was going to turn out. That kept me going.

Jennifer was quick to point out the bigger issue, that I not only love my work but it's the only job I know. I've been a photographer for my entire adult life. Since this life-changing event, I wasn't sure if I'd be able to continue doing it anymore. "Now you're really put to the test," she told me. "Who are you and what will you do with your life without your camera?"

CHAPTER 12

I t was a huge question. That day, I came home and feverishly started scrubbing the dried blood off my black canvas camera bag. It was the first day since the accident that I truly began to cry. Why was everyone always challenging the idea that I'd get my life back? With tears of frustration running down my face, I decided I hadn't come this far just to give up. Maybe my doctors were right, and I'd have to forge a new life that wouldn't include scuba diving, rock climbing, or adventuring around the world with my cameras. But before I accepted that, I had to know I'd done everything I could to reclaim the life I loved.

I was a determined and dedicated photographer. I especially loved the dirt, the grit, and the chaos of third world travel. I lived for the interaction with the people I met and that wonderful collision of light and subject, the feeling I got when I knew

I'd made a good image. I was married to my work, for richer or for poorer, in sickness and in health, for better or worse (I'd certainly run that whole gamut). It's often not an easy road, but I was devoted to it.

When they saw the peripatetic way I lived, people sometimes asked me what I was running away from. To my mind, it was an odd question—for me, it was more like I was running *to* something. I was always working when I traveled. I wasn't a tourist—my work gave me a sense of direction and focus, and took me beneath the surface of a culture. It was more than just observing from the outside. Becoming immersed in foreign lands had helped me develop a strong inner confidence and kinship with humanity. I had always felt comfortable wherever I was in the world, but I felt now that I was bobbing along in unchartered waters. It was time to reconnect with that deeper sense of self.

I put my camera bag away. "Jennifer's right," I thought. I couldn't help but wonder what my new role in life would be. It felt as though I was defined by this incident: I was the woman who'd been hit by a bus. The events of my life were now compartmentalized into before the accident and after the accident.

I had no doubt that what I'd learned as a yoga practitioner and meditator—how to focus on my breathing—was what saved me. And this became the foundation on which I would base my recovery. I sat on my bed and closed my eyes. I tried to empty my mind and not let it get caught up in a downward spiral. As usual, my thoughts bounced through my brain like popcorn. The Tibetan lamas call this "monkey mind."

Deep breath. Emptiness.

"I am here, just sitting."

This intensive Buddhist meditation technique has no mantra—the breath is used as a point of focus. I let my thoughts rise and fall as they would, without getting caught up in the narrative.

"My knee really hurts. I wonder if I'm doing permanent nerve damage? What if I'm actually crippling myself by sitting for this long without moving?

"Fear is just a thought. Let it go. Breathe deeply.

"It's such a beautiful day. Why am I inside? Maybe I should be out walking on the beach.

"Don't get lost in the story . . .

"I should be working and getting those photos edited. Maybe I can take a walk later. I'm starving. What should I make for lunch? I have so many things to do. Why am I wasting my time with this? I should be doing something more constructive."

The "shoulds" danced around my head like little devils with pitchforks.

"Hey you, get back here."

I focused on each inhalation and exhalation.

Always I came back to the stability of my breath. My anchor.

As in those first moments in Laos, I now lay on my bed in my room and used meditation to help manage my all-encompassing pain—breathing into it with awareness, and observing it. At times one pinpoint of intensity would overshadow the rest. Was it sharp? Deep? Throbbing? Was it in a broad or specific area? I worked to dissolve the grip of tension, to imagine it melting and dissipating throughout my body. I envisioned it as a color—sometimes a searing red or piercing yellow—and then I'd wash it away, far away, with a wave of cool cerulean blue on a cloudless summer day.

Buddhism is the backbone of human existence in Tibet, Burma, Cambodia, Thailand, and elsewhere in Asia. Their devotion to it is incorporated into practically every daily activity. The value of this philosophy is evident in the way people from those countries have survived ordeals of exile, genocide, and imprisonment with humor and determination and an ability to keep things in perspective. They have managed to retain a profound sense of purpose in their cultures.

A desire to learn more about this impressive belief system inspired me to visit Bodhgaya, India, where I began attending three-week meditation retreats in the mid-1980s. My mind drifted to one of the first times I went there. Bodhgaya, an eighteen-hour train ride from Delhi, is the village where, twenty-five hundred years ago, the seeker Siddhartha Gautama planted himself in meditation under the bodhi tree until he reached the truly awakened state as an enlightened Buddha. Bodhgaya is home to a concentration of temples from every Buddhist country and lineage imaginable, including Zen from Japan; Therevada from Thailand, Sri Lanka, Korea, and Taiwan; as well as Tibetan Buddhism. When I was there, cows sauntered along the streets amid a sea of people and a cacophony of vehicles. Teahouses served sweet milky cardamom tea, the acrid smell from their stoves permeating the air. Tailors couldn't sew their handmade meditation cushions fast enough to supply the inexhaustible stream of yogis striving to obtain enlightenment during their travels through India.

It was Beru Khyentse Rinpoche, a high Tibetan lama with a monastery in Bodhgaya, who stressed the importance of this area to me. "This is the land Buddha first blessed, now the land blesses man. The ground has accumulated energy from years of meditation, and many masters have come here to be enlightened. Laypeople come to this holy place to light butter lamps, to pray, and to perform prostrations to achieve merit for success and purification. For you see, all actions performed here, good or bad, are multiplied hundreds of times." This, I decided, made a very good reason to be on my best bodhisattva-like behavior.

It didn't take me long to falter. Christopher, the bearded English meditation teacher who was leading the retreat in the Thai temple, caught me outside the monastery photographing the hundreds of Tibetan monks who had gathered for a ceremony under the bodhi tree where the Buddha himself had once sat. The scene had been too visually enticing for me to avoid: the gathering of monks chanting prayers, prostrating before the tree, lighting candles.

Christopher took me aside and told me off. "I saw you out there shooting. You know you're not supposed to leave the monastery grounds. I realize you're struggling with staying here, but what are you willing to give up to find what you're looking for?" I was taken aback. Did he mean give up my camera? I could never imagine going somewhere without the intent to photograph. It was my reason for being.

Christopher had been a journalist himself, covering famines and war. Questioning such human suffering led him to abandon his profession and become a monk in Thailand. Now he was based in England, leading meditation retreats around the world. He was clear, direct, and had a biting yet insightful sense of delivery regarding the Buddhist teachings.

To this day, I have never entered a meditation retreat without an inner struggle. I question taking time away from photographing and working. Is it really a worthwhile use of my time to sit on a cushion all day when there are pictures to be shot, photos to be edited? For the same reason it is always difficult for me to take a vacation—no matter where in the world I travel I want to document it. In the end, though, I always feel more creative and open after a few days of calming my mind and letting the mud in my brain settle. It's not usually an easy process getting to that point, but I've realized that if I let go and listen, I'll learn something.

Every evening during the retreat, Christopher would give a candlelit talk after dinner. During one he reminded us of the Four Noble Truths. The first is that there is suffering in life. "Things don't always go the way we'd like them to. The world was not created to suit the whim of the human mind—and for that we should be eternally grateful. It's for us to learn to accept what is."

He addressed the second noble truth, the cause of suffering as ignorance and attachment. We attach to our thoughts, our bodies and minds, and think, "This is who I am." But really life is so fluid it's an illusion. Our feelings and emotions shift and change from one minute to the next, eventually our bodies deteriorate. All of this around us is impermanent.

The third noble truth, he pointed out, speaks of obtaining the wisdom to free ourselves from this distorted concept of who we think we are: to truly understand the nature of life, to recognize the boundless love within ourselves and those around us. This will free us from suffering.

"And it is the fourth noble truth, these meditation techniques, which are the path to helping us obtain this liberation."

I was more than aware of how much these insights had already helped me in my view of the world. Meditating had brought a profound awareness and clarity to my life just as it brought vision to my work. It encouraged me to become more absorbed and engaged with the people I photograph, while not becoming too emotionally involved in their personal dramas. It has aided me in calmly processing the intensity of what I see from behind the lens of my camera. Surprisingly, it's helped me to make better pictures. The concept of letting go of ego has also helped me to keep perspective in my competitive business by not getting caught up in measuring my self-worth by whether I got my photos published or not.

One thing has always been extremely tough—the return to

home life in the States. Sometimes when I come back from developing countries I am plagued by the dichotomy between our lives and the way most of the world lives. We have so many choices. I get overwhelmed just trying to decide which laundry soap to choose in the supermarket. How could I have so much when so many have so little? This awareness has brought me a daily appreciation for even the simplest things I do have: a hot shower, a soft bed, food on the table.

So much of what I do, the course I decide to follow, is based on quieting my mind enough to hear the inner voice that directs me to the next step. We are all on individual paths, and we just need to listen to the stillness in our heart to know what our life's purpose is. The signs are all around us if we pay attention and slow down enough to become aware of them. We all have this ability; it just gets overwhelmed by what society dictates and feelings of what we "ought" to be doing. If I didn't create circumstances that let the murkiness in my mind and my heart settle, I'm not sure I would be able to hear those choices so clearly.

In Bodhgaya other questions troubled me too. One day I approached Fred, a Swiss teacher who was helping Christopher lead the retreat. "It's difficult for me to not want to hold on to the people and things that mean so much to me in my life," I told him. "Yet I don't want to become totally emotionally removed. What is the difference between detachment and unattachment?"

Fred took a pen and held it downward in his clenched hand. When he let go, it fell to the floor. "Unattachment," said Fred.

He then took the pen and rested it in the open palm of his hand. "Letting go," he said.

Then, with his typical sense of humor, he added one more insight. "There were two priests who were smokers, but they weren't sure if it was all right with the Vatican, so they both wrote to the Pope. One got the okay, the other didn't. Amazed, the one who didn't asked the other what he wrote. 'I wrote and asked him if it's all right to smoke while I prayed,' the one priest complained. 'Now what did you ask?'

"The other priest replied, 'I wrote and asked him if it was okay to pray while I smoke.'

"So you see, Alison," Fred said laughing, "it's all how you ask the question. Letting go doesn't necessarily mean getting rid of."

After those weeks of sitting and inquiring, I finally understood what Christopher meant by asking what was I willing to give up. It was the first time I really saw who I was without that camera. No ego. I wasn't defined by being a woman, a photographer, a sister, or a daughter. I just was. And I was able to feel that being to the inner core. I finally got it. I didn't have to give up photography. I had to give up my attachment to it.

Still, every year Christopher continued to lock up my equipment for the duration of the retreat.

A shooting jolt in my lower back brought me back to the present, and I shifted my weight to get comfortable. While photographing my way around the world I had often found myself in situations that tested my limits. Thinking back to those introspective times in India, I realized that every challenge I'd been confronted with in my life had been preparing me not only for surviving this traumatic event but to finding the strength from within to pull myself forward.

I opened my eyes and took a deep breath.

"All right," I thought. "Let's see what you're really capable of."

CHAPTER 13

First I needed my wits back: strength of mind for strength of body. Three months after the accident I took a decisive step toward recovery: I ceremoniously dumped my hard-hitting arsenal of painkillers down the toilet. This might mean never a moment of respite from the blinding discomfort I felt throughout my body, but I was determined to learn other ways to keep it at bay. I wanted the fog to lift.

I bought every book I could find on alternative healing and began incorporating meditation, guided imagery, homeopathic medicine, and even hypnosis into my rehabilitation. I tried magnets for my back and cupping, an ancient Chinese practice wherein heated glass cups are suctioned onto the skin, drawing the blood to the surface to stimulate circulation. Moxibustion— using a heated stick to warm the surface of my back—worked in a similar way. In addition to reflexology, I eventually added yoga and Pilates, along with massage, Rolfing, and chiropractic work. I also tried different herbs and extracts. I took noni and glucosamine for my joints, melatonin and valerian for sleep, and arnica for my hematoma, which was taking months to fade.

I had come to rely on acupuncture too, to treat everything from my unrelenting insomnia to pain. During my initial visits, Byron, my acupuncturist, usually inserted a number of needles into my body and always one into my foot. As he twirled it around I grimaced. I eventually asked him what it was for. He explained that energy meridians pass though different points of our bodies and affect our health. Each energy channel affects a different internal organ. By stimulating that external part with a needle, the negative energy is redirected from the internal organ that's in pain. "This particular point affects the spleen," he told me. Indeed, I was still recovering from a lacerated spleen.

Four tedious months after the accident I had regained enough strength to take short steps for fairly long periods of time, albeit with great difficulty, with crutches or a cane, and a very lopsided limp. Still, I was walking.

My mind too was much clearer now. I studied medical texts to understand my diagnosis and to comprehend the repercussions of my surgeries. I spent so much time reading these books over steaming hot bowls of *phở* in the little Vietnamese restaurant next door to the hospital, the couple that ran it kept referring to me as a doctor. I took copious notes and went armed to my health appointments with informed questions.

During this time, I went to my dentist for what should have been a relatively straightforward replacement of an old filling. But it seemed that nothing would be easy. As I left her office and the novocaine started to wear off, it felt as if the drill was continuing to work its way through my jaw. By the time I got home it was as if a lightning bolt had hit me in the side of the face. The excruciating sharpness brought me to my knees on the living room floor. "What now?" I thought. In that moment, all the broken bones I'd experienced paled in comparison to this. I called the dentist in tears, begging her to pull the tooth or whatever needed to be done. Nothing she recommended calmed the pain, not the bag of frozen peas or secret stash of painkillers, and the office was about to close for the weekend.

In desperation I went to Byron so he could treat me with acupuncture. He inserted one small needle directly into my toe. The effect was so immediate it took me by surprise. It no longer felt as if an ice pick was twisting its way through my jaw. It wasn't permanent but at least there was a reprieve, and the blinding jabs were brought somewhat under control.

As it seemed somewhat inconvenient to walk around with a needle in my toe, I went to see my doctor first thing Monday morning. He recommended a neurologist who presented me with a diagnosis.

"I believe you have trigeminal neuralgia, or tic douloureux," he said. He told me that the shooting twinges in my face are affected by the trigeminal nerve, one of the largest in the head. Each heartbeat causes the enlarged blood vessel to press on the nerve, wearing away its insulation. "It possibly could have been caused by head trauma from the collision then aggravated by the dental work. Trigeminal neuralgia is often considered one of the most painful conditions in medicine." I decided that if acupuncture could calm suffering that severe, I was sold. He then prescribed Neurontin, an antiseizure medication. In this case, as with all my healing, both Eastern and Western medicine would play a role in my recuperation.

I had first been exposed to alternative healing in the 1980s while living among Tibetan communities in Asia and working on my photo book *The Spirit of Tibet*.

Tibet has held an allure for me ever since I was a child. I remember being in a museum in London and seeing the ornate robes of the old Buddhist lamas in electric blue, crimson, and gold silk brocade, the arms spread out to reveal exotic symbols and patterns, and saying to myself, "I'm going to go there one day." Despite their foreignness, they seemed so familiar.

I was thrilled when I got my job in Nepal, which brought me closer to realizing my dream of getting to Tibet. What I didn't fully comprehend was the severity of the atrocities that had befallen this isolated country since the 1959 Chinese infiltration.

Meeting so many refugees is what led me to documenting Tibetan life in exile and the tales of their diaspora.

I wasn't feeling my best by the time I reached Dharamsala, home to the Dalai Lama and thousands of relocated Tibetans. Months of traveling in India were starting to take their toll.

"You do look awful," said my friend Jigme, a Tibetan monk who was helping translate interviews for my book. "Have you looked in a mirror recently?"

As far as I was concerned, in India mirrors were to be avoided at all cost, and a quick visual check reminded me why. My skin was sallow and there were dark circles under my eyes. Even more of a concern was that had I recently begun coughing up disturbing dark phlegm. Could it be tuberculosis? I never would have tolerated being so ill at home and realized Jigme was right—it was time for a professional diagnosis.

Jigme encouraged me to see Dr. Yeshi Dhonden, the local Tibetan doctor. I had my doubts. If I had something as serious as TB, I wanted to see a *real* doctor. That morning I traipsed down to Delek Hospital and went through all the standard testing.

"You have worms," the lab technician told me as he peered through his microscope. "It seems that you must have had them for many weeks, as they have become so bad they are now in your lungs." The concept of billions of hungry worms feeding on my insides was more than I could bear.

"Give me anything, just get rid of these things right away!"

I pleaded. The doctor handed me a cellophane packet of small white pills.

While heading back up to town, Jigme looked crestfallen. "You mean, if you take these pills they kill all the worms in your body?" he asked.

"That's right," I said, greedily popping a couple of the tablets into my mouth as we walked up the hill. "Apparently within three days." I was hoping it would be much sooner.

"But they're living creatures. You'll be killing many lives," Jigme protested. "Once, in our monastery, all the monks contracted worms, but no one would take the medicine to kill them. It's bad karma. If you take the medicine, you must have a puja, or religious ritual, for the lives of the worms you're killing."

I groaned. Not only did I feel sick, now I felt guilty. But what he said made sense as far as Buddhist beliefs are concerned, and I knew if I were to live within this culture and really try be a part of it then I should respect their ways.

At Jigme's insistence, that afternoon we worked our way into Dr. Dhonden's crowded waiting room.

"Hey, this is just like my doctor's office during flu season," I joked. Jigme gave me a flat smile, and I sensed that he was still upset with the idea that I was annihilating living beings within my body. I was feeling pretty queasy with the idea myself as I slid down to sit on the floor.

Tibetans of all ages, from the smallest of babies feeding at their mother's breasts to old people diligently spinning prayer wheels, sat with an air of contented patience, apparently unconcerned by the nonexistence of waiting room magazines. The sound of their murmuring prayers hummed like a hive of bees. I was surprised at how many Westerners were dispersed throughout the room. A very pregnant couple with German accents sat chatting in the corner, reading through a pamphlet explaining which Tibetan medicines to take during pregnancy. A pale young traveler sporting a long ponytail sat slumped against the wall, his eyes staring vacantly at the floor. Occasionally, Dr. Dhonden's assistant would surface from behind the closed door, odd-sounding names from around the world rolling off his tongue with surprising ease. It was obvious that this type of crowd was the norm.

Finally we were called into the room. It didn't look much like a doctor's office. There was just a desk, a leather chair, and a table. I was immediately attracted to Dr. Dhonden, a sweet elflike man with enormous ears, who was dressed in long maroon monk's robes. Able to speak very few words of English, Dr. Dhonden warmly took my hand and wished me a boisterous *tashi delek,* a Tibetan greeting.

His assistant translated as Dr. Dhonden agreed to perform a routine checkup, resting his three left fingers with varying pressure on the pulse of my right wrist. I felt his first finger only lightly press the skin, the second enough to feel the flesh, and the third enough to feel the bone underneath it. He then switched to my left wrist. Dr. Dhonden commented that my pulse was the hardest one to find he'd had all day.

"Why, because it's so weak?" I asked worriedly.

"No, because of all your bracelets," he chuckled heartily.

"Each division of your wrist reads a specific organ of the body," he explained through the translator. The doctor and assistant then had a brief exchange in Tibetan. "Dr. Dhonden says your pulse is knotty, then flat. He says you have bad worms."

I looked at both men incredulously. "You can tell that from my pulse?" I asked in awe. My first inclination was to think that someone had already told him my previous diagnosis. But he had come to his own conclusion. Admiring the patience of this doctor whose waiting room was as crowded as a Macy's sale, I listened as he explained more about the Tibetan approach to medicine.

"In the Tibetan system, which is mainly derived from Indian Buddhist medicine, we believe that whether we are physically healthy or not, basically all of us harbor illness; it is ever present in a dormant form.

"As with most holistic medicine, the mind-body connection is the most important element in the healing practice. The smallest imbalance can produce disease. We treat these disturbances through a change in diet and herbal medicine: herbal incense, medicinal herbal baths, and herbal pills."

I breathed a sigh of relief. This was certainly less severe than the other Tibetan treatments I had witnessed. On a visit to a Tibetan hospital I had photographed a monk, a young boy who was being treated for a migraine headache. The nurse brought out the "golden hammer," a small tool that had been heated in a fire. They

Top of the Dolma-La Pass. Despite the bitter cold, I stopped here to tie prayer flags at the peak of my thirty-three-mile circumambulation of Mount Kailash, Tibet.

I have been going to Tibet nearly every year for the last twenty years to document that endangered culture. Here I am pictured with a nomad girl in a remote region of Eastern Tibet.

The Dalai Lama stops to bless his Indian guard while walking from his home to his office. Dharamsala, India.

Dodging bullets while covering the revolution in Kathmandu, Nepal. The photographer is unknown; this image was removed from the wall of the police station in Kathmandu.

Three years after my accident I got back on the local bus, similar to the one that had crashed, to return to Luang Prabang in Laos. Unbelievably, during our journey this bus clipped another one.

Khamthat Chanthamougkhong, the young man who sewed up my arm with what resembled an upholstery needle, using no painkillers or anesthesia. He was instrumental in stopping me from bleeding to death.

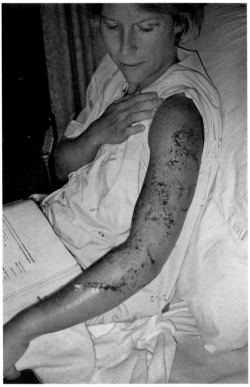

My arm, in between dressings, with hundreds of stitches two weeks after the accident. Aek Udon Hospital, Udon Thani, Thailand.

Roel and Meia Snelder, the Dutch couple who were also in the accident. Roel had proposed to Meia the day before. Aek Udon Hospital, Udon Thani, Thailand.

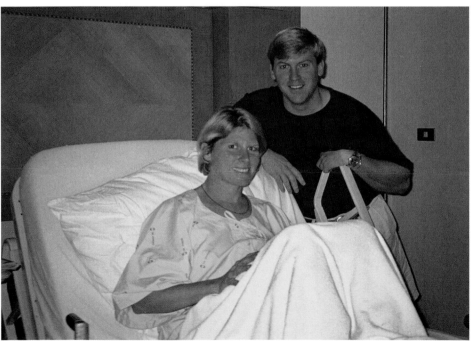

With my brother, Andrew, two weeks after the accident, celebrating the fact that I am finally out of intensive care. Around my neck, I'm still wearing the red protection cord given to me in Tibet by the Karmapa Lama. Aek Udon Hospital, Udon Thani, Thailand.

Dr. Bunsom Santithamnont, who saved my life on the operating table and subsequently performed numerous surgeries on me during my weeks in Thailand. At the time of this visit it had been three years since the accident and it is the first time he is seeing me standing up and walking. Aek Udon Hospital, Udon Thani, Thailand.

On a return visit to Kasi Clinic, now expanded into Kasi Hospital, I had an emotional reunion with those who helped me after my accident. Khamthat Chanthamougkhong, who initially sewed up my arm, is on the far left, and Dr. Seng is third from the left with the team nurses. Kasi, Laos.

Happier times. With my nieces, Claire, Erin, and Hannah, at their home in Denver, Colorado.

Me on top of Mount Kilimanjaro; the dawning of a new day, a new decade, a new life, and my fortieth birthday!

The Dalai Lama greeting me during one of my many visits to Dharamsala, India.

placed it against his skin, and as they touched each specific point on his face and head he squirmed in agony as it left searing brand marks. The next day might have been even worse. This time, the nurse brought out the "golden needle." I could barely watch as the thick handcrafted metal point was inserted deep through the crown of his head where the two parts of the skull conjoin. At that point I couldn't help but speak up, "Excuse me, but I have some aspirin in my bag if anyone wants to try that."

"Sometimes patients don't respond to long periods of medication," continued Dr. Dhonden. "When this happens, these disorders are sometimes thought to be the influence of interfering spirits. In order to free the patient from these disorders, the spirit must be exorcised by a shaman, and the disease will be cured."

I had witnessed these shamans in their trances as they performed on their patients when I photographed a healing ritual in a Tibetan refugee camp in Nepal. The shaman, a seemingly unassuming man, entered the room, and once he was dressed in flowing colorful robes and a tall wooden hat his personality immediately changed. Once this elaborate headgear, decorated with Buddhist imagery, was placed on his head he was considered possessed by the healing deity and his powers are enabled. The shaman, no longer the quiet man I had initially met, went into a mesmerized trance by chanting Buddhist prayers in a high-pitched voice accompanied by his frantically clanging bell and the incessant beat of his small drum.

In this particular instance, the possessed shaman surprised me by suddenly jumping out of my picture frame, screaming that I had "dis-ease," or lack of ease, in my body. He threw up my shirt and proceeded to suck on my stomach, spitting huge, unappealing globs of black mucous into a cup. Healing or parlor trick, I wasn't sure, but the woman of the house swore he had extricated a coin from her child's stomach in exactly the same way.

"Buddhists believe in rebirth, and many of these types of disorders are attributed to negative actions committed in past lives," said Dr. Dhonden. "When that karma ripens, the disease manifests itself in the present lifetime, and it can often prove fatal."

Armed with that knowledge, I followed Dr. Dhonden outside as he performed the next procedure, a urinalysis. I sat on the concrete steps and watched as he began to whip my urine with a small wooden stick, apparently observing the bubbles. With all the intensity of a chemist, he told me that he was noting the color of the urine, the odor, the steam rising from it, and looking for any sediment. Believing that urine reflects the internal state of the body like a mirror, a good Tibetan doctor can often diagnose and prescribe a cure by urine analysis alone.

When we returned inside, the doctor also checked my tongue, my eyes, and my stomach. There was another verbal exchange between doctor and assistant.

"By the way," said the translator, in the typical offhand way Tibetans often have of phrasing significant news, "the doctor says you also have beginning stages of hepatitis. Your liver is very inflamed. But he has good medicine for this."

"We have a very high success rate in treating involved illnesses like this," Dr. Dhonden explained. At this point I was beginning to feel that I was getting more than I had bargained for. He went on to say that he believed in Western medicine for quickly stopping certain diseases—fever, tuberculosis—and painkillers for emergency cases. The advantage of Tibetan medicine is that it can treat the source of the illness rather than just the symptoms.

With that he handed me a variety of small plastic bags containing the medicine: shiny brown balls that resembled rabbit droppings. One bag contained a few "precious pills," hard balls of herbs and minerals that were delicately wrapped in blue silk, tied with colored string, and sealed with wax. He showed me how to crush the pills and swallow them with hot water, which I was to continue to do at designated times of the day. They tasted bitter and gritty.

"I believe that love and compassion for fellow human beings is a strong part of our Tibetan culture and necessary for a practitioner of medicine. I try to incorporate this into my life, my healing practice, and everything I do," Dr. Dhonden said.

After trying to imagine my health-care professionals in America uttering this idea, I told Dr. Dhonden that I admired his philosophy and asked how he got involved in medicine.

He told me that his parents sent him to a monastery to become a monk at age six, a common practice in Tibet before the Chinese invasion. By age eleven he had entered medical school, and only two years later passed the exam, which entailed reciting the fourteen hundred pages of the four medical tantras. At thirteen he was admitted to his first medical-training class.

At twenty-two, he received his medical degree and left Lhasa to practice in his home district, where an army of twenty thousand soldiers greeted him during the Chinese takeover. Eight years later there was an uprising against the Chinese and fighting broke out in Lhasa. "As a monk I couldn't fight. When the Dalai Lama left Tibet in 1959, I knew it was time for me to leave also."

Thousands of Tibetans fled to Dharamsala to be near the Dalai Lama at his new residence in exile. Yeshi Dhonden was immediately appointed the personal physician of the Tibetan leader, checking his pulse with each sunrise. Dr. Dhonden's long days were spent visiting the makeshift tents and treating many of the new refugees. Due to the drastic change in climate and close living conditions, tuberculosis and other diseases spread rampantly. The severity of the situation inspired him to open his own practice in Dharamsala, seeing dozens of patients a day. If this doctor was good enough for the Dalai Lama, I decided, he was good enough for me.

Dr. Dhonden explained that the idea of Tibetan medicine is to combine the treatment with a positive healing attitude from within the patient. Sickness provides an opportunity for us to grow, to see where we have gone out of balance and to advance spiritually. It is a practice for developing compassion, to release oneself from the aversion to pain and unhappiness.

I had no idea how much this advice would affect me in my later healing experiences. Although I utilize Western medicine,

I am also a firm believer in the importance, not just of Tibetan medicine, but of all holistic medical practice. I can attest to the fact that my hepatitis never advanced any further after my herbal treatment, and I was able to resume my strength and continue to work throughout India for many months. But I also took the medicine given to me by the doctor at Delek Hospital, and within a short time managed to clear my lungs.

And by the way, I did have a puja to atone for killing those worms.

A decade later I had occasion to learn a lot more about nontraditional healing when I spent time with shamans in the Amazon rain forest. Right after graduate school I had been invited by a San Francisco–based pharmaceutical company to document Tom, their ethnobotanist and medical doctor, and Peter, an anthropologist, who were heading into the jungle in search of medicinal plants to bring back to the United States to test their healing qualities.

When we arrived in Iquitos, Peru, I was a little dismayed when I saw the empty carcass of an old fishing boat that had been arranged for our travels. It lay on its side with a huge hole in the bow, not even floating. Unfortunately, this seemed to be the only boat available in Iquitos that was spacious enough for our research and potentially durable enough to travel the two thousand miles we planned to cover.

Determined to expedite our departure, we equipped ourselves

with five gallons of the cheapest and least offensive red and gray paint we could find and shocked the owner by showing up to work on the boat ourselves. For nearly two weeks we waded through the bureaucratic wasteland of paperwork necessary to obtain the various permits to visit the isolated places we were heading into and, as is the custom there, bribed officials until we could bribe no more.

I had to admit that I really had my doubts as we boarded the old boat for the lengthy voyage with no radio on board, no fire extinguisher, and no life jackets.

We finally managed to get on the river two days before Christmas. It was my birthday, and in the dark of night we pulled over to some lights on shore to see if we could buy a beer. I was the one who first noticed something odd about the place.

We had landed at a leper colony. No ice-cold Molson here, but they enthusiastically shared their *chicha* with us. The local women, whose saliva causes the starch to ferment into a kind of wine, masticate manioc root to make this rather distinctive beverage. It tasted of rancid yogurt.

The air was thick with mosquitoes, and because we slept outside in hammocks on the deck of the boat, we got no respite from them. For some reason they were most attracted to me. Undeterred by military jungle juice insect repellent and dense (hot!) clothing, they imperviously seared holes in our oppressive mosquito netting. I was miserable.

My blistering wounds actually made for great conversation

with the locals as we cruised down the river. For most of the Indians in the Yagua and Mayoruna villages we came across, I must
have been one of the more unusual women they had ever seen.
Curiosity about the pus-filled welts all over my body overshad-
owed any at my white skin and blonde hair.

Leaving Tom and Peter to their pursuits, I obsessively questioned the locals about what they used to treat bug attacks.
Surely, I figured, they must know better than any of us. The
predominant choice seemed to be rubbing lemon juice onto the
festering bites. So, feeling like a ceviche salad, I devoutly rubbed
citrus on my appendages four times a day. The searing acidic
anguish was similar, I'm sure, to rubbing rock salt into open
wounds. This process succeeded only in inducing my blisters to
become septic, and a fever soon set in. So much for that particular
local cure—when the staph infection started eating at my flesh, I
opted for antibiotics.

In more than a month of floating along in our rickety boat, with
Peru on one side, Brazil on the other, we had covered hundreds of
miles. We were delighted to have finally reached the elusive Matsés tribe. Once ashore, we cut our way through the dense jungle
with machetes, our clothes soaked through from the muggy heat.
Pablo, our helpful shaman, led the way.

"These leaves are used topically for treating chicken pox,"
Pablo said, pointing out various plants, trees, and vines. "The sap
from this plant is extracted for treating herpes. The heart of palm
from this tree is boiled and drunk for treating diabetes. These

leaves are applied to the chest for treating a cold." He stopped to show us a thorny vine called *uña de gato,* or cat's claw. "We use this to treat dysentery, fevers, arthritis, and stomach ulcers."

At one point Pablo stopped and broke off a branch that appeared to be sweating. He convinced me to let him drip its seeping droplets into my eye. My eyes never felt so clear and refreshed—it was like I'd had a dose of Visine, only fifty times stronger. The deeper we walked through the green cathedral of trees, the lungs of the planet, the more I came to admire the Amazon peoples' knowledge about this natural pharmacopoeia. Maybe this place could indeed house a cure for cancer, diabetes, even AIDS.

The Matsés believe themselves to be descendants of the jaguar. To represent the hunting aspect of their nature they wear jagged toothlike tattoos, which follow the outline of their jaws like railroad tracks. Small holes rim their noses, through which they once proudly poked "cat whiskers," until informed by Christian missionaries that this was not considered an appropriate practice. Not long after, polyester gym shorts replaced penis sheaths. A shaman from one of the neighboring Yagua tribes comically shimmied up trees in a ruffle-fronted tuxedo shirt.

Despite such physical changes, the Amazon Indians still continued to live much as they had for hundreds of years. They moved through the world with a profound sense of place and purpose. Women foraged for food, and babies grew up playing in the jungle. Men still hunted wild boar with poisoned arrows and blowguns and took their dugout canoes out onto the river to fish with harpoons.

On our last night in the village, Pablo invited us to try *sapo*, a secretion emitted from a frog's sweat glands. The Matsés scrape the snotty-looking stuff onto a stick and let it dry until they're ready to use it. After a lengthy ceremony, they burn it into their skin, inducing uncontrollable vomiting and defecating. Once the body has cleared itself in this way, the Matsés believe the hunter receives a clear vision of where the animals lie in wait. Sapo is also said to increase stamina and energy.

Clearly, we were going to be that evening's entertainment. The whole village had piled onto our boat to view us entering this altered state. There was tangible excitement in the air as Pablo began heating up the slime-covered little twig.

"You sure know how to show a girl a good time," I laughed weakly to my companions as Pablo burned through a small layer of skin on each of our arms with a thick hand-rolled cigarette. As he leaned over, I noticed hundreds of burn marks riding up and down his arm. "Ah, a sapo junkie," I thought.

Violently purging in front of fifty-odd people was not high on my list of desires, and I opted for one hit rather than the customary five. As soon as Pablo dabbed the vile-looking ball of slime into the fresh burn, my arm began to tingle with an unrelenting fiery sensation. My pulse was racing and I felt as though I were trapped inside a closed, airless elevator. I began to sweat profusely. Tom's head seemed to be throbbing, or was it my own eyeballs? I flicked the ball of mucus off my arm, hoping the nausea would subside, but it only slightly reduced the hammering in my brain.

My stomach was churning, and I tried desperately not to think about the wild boar dinner one of Pablo's wives had cooked for us earlier that evening. Peter wasn't as successful; I heard him heaving over the side of the boat. "These people must have hearts like racehorses," I thought, to do multiple sapo hits at one time.

Eventually, I crawled over to the bench to lie down. Martha, Pablo's first wife, flashed me a smile, displaying giant teeth outlined in the blue Matsés tribe tattoo. Martha took my head on her lap and stroked my hair. Only a half hour earlier I had been laughing and joking with her. I wasn't hallucinating, but everything suddenly seemed to be pulsating with a surreal intensity. That said, I also found the experience extremely bonding, as all those around me had been in this space before and knew exactly what we were going through. They let us know that we were the first white folks they had ever invited to take part in this ritual and we were honored. Still, I was glad when the locals grew bored with our wimpy reactions and filed off the boat.

The next morning my queasiness was worse than ever. In addition to discomfort from the previous night's experience, I'd felt as though something was stuck in my throat ever since the fish lunch the day before. Tom looked down my gullet and was amazed to see a fish bone tightly wedged inside, setting off my gag reflex.

"Wow, that's really lodged in there. You're going to have to wait until we get back to Iquitos to numb the area and surgically remove it," he said. But I was desperate. My throat was swollen and every swallow was torture. Afraid that I would starve to death, I begged Tom to try to remove the obstruction. Using surgical forceps nearly the length of my forearm, Tom's steady arm managed to extract from my throat a spiny bone the size of a cigarette lighter.

With nothing more than a severe sore throat, I was now well enough to join the entourage heading into the jungle. Tom and Peter had collected a record twelve plant specimens by late afternoon. Pablo was convinced that their successful hunting trip was due to the sapo from the night before. Meanwhile, Martha and Mashu, another of Pablo's wives, had followed us into the rain forest, and Martha beckoned me to accompany her in the direction of a distant chopping sound. Giggling, she suddenly raced barefoot through a teeming river of giant leaf-toting red ants marching as though on a mission across the jungle floor. I was apprehensive about crossing their path, even in my heavy hiking boots.

I was astounded when I discovered the source of the hollow echo. There was tiny Mashu, felling an eighty-foot tree with a small hatchet. Martha plopped herself down on a fallen log, and I gladly did the same. The familiar buzz of mosquitoes soon surrounded us.

Noticing my discomfort, Martha began plucking leaves from a nearby palm and quickly wove an exquisite little fan. Smiling, she handed it to me—so this was her answer to dealing with those unrelenting pests. This intimate gesture touched me deeply, not only for the obvious usefulness of the gift, but also for her shy attempt at communicating.

With swift, flicking hand gestures, Martha then began nimbly crafting a large basket from green palm fronds. Barely flinching, she looked up distractedly as Mashu's large tree came crashing down at her side. Succulent, ripe palm fruits now lay at her fingertips, and she quickly began tossing them into her newly made basket. Pausing briefly, she stooped to cleverly weave a small scoop that served to expedite the process.

Tom's worried call snapped me out of my fascination with the foraging scene.

"I'm over here with Mashu and Martha!" I yelled.

This sent Martha into lighthearted amusement, and she showed me how the women communicate with their men while working in the jungle—a deep-throated moaning sound. In the distance, I heard Pablo echo a reply. The women and I laughed as I tried to mimic their guttural noises. The men had no problem finding us at that point. Tom joked that he regretted having pulled that fish bone out of my throat.

Ready to head back, the two women hoisted the heavy baskets onto their backs, looping a strong vine around their foreheads for support. Pablo joined us, happily scampering along empty-handed, except for his long machete. His third wife also followed along, carrying their small baby slung on her back, much the same way the other women were lugging their baskets. The baby was sick with a cold, and Martha occasionally stopped to pick medicinal plants to stuff into the little girl's shirt next to her chest—the rain forest's answer to Vicks VapoRub.

With multiple wives, Pablo seemed to have fathered nearly every child in the village (forty at last count), and we were always sure to have a full entourage whenever we went into the jungle to collect specimens.

Even Pablo's young children were quick to loop vines around their skinny little ankles and shimmy up to the tops of trees to retrieve specific plants that they had spotted. Mimicking their father, the boys scurried through the forest in delight, shooting at small birds and rodents with their tiny bows and arrows. The youngsters had been banned from playing with their homemade weapons for some time, Pablo explained, because they had a tendency to shoot at all the village dogs and chickens. We looked over to where the boys were sticking their legs deep into the giant red ant hills, daring one another to stay immersed as long as possible.

"Very naughty boys," Pablo stated without much conviction.

At the end of the day we returned to the river and tentatively bathed from the edge of a small wooden raft where the women washed their clothes. The river held crocodiles and candiru, small parasitic fish whose sole purpose on this planet is to swim up one's urethra and lodge there until surgically removed. This was enough to deter us from a full immersion.

Back on the boat we prepared for our long passage back down the Amazon to Iquitos. I finished bagging my rolls of film while Tom and Peter gloated over their booty, labeling over fifty species of plants they'd collected on the trip. The sun set, giving the air an illusion of cooling, although the dusk really just marked a change of shift for the ever-present insects. As our boat cleaved the rich chocolate-colored waters, a human-sounding gasp emerged from the depths of the river. I peered over the side. There was a struggle for breath, followed by another. I was worried; was someone drowning? In the descending darkness I could make out small white spouts of spray. It was a school of pink river dolphins, at least twenty of them, leaping in harmonious rhythm. Playfully swimming in circles around the boat, they emitted a loud chorus of breathless pants in unison. It was as if they knew we were leaving, as if they had come to say good-bye.

CHAPTER 14

my friends continued to play a huge part in my recovery and were determined to help me walk properly again. The warm weather arrived with spring, and when I had the energy, they would take me on my favorite drives to visit Bay Area beaches and smell the invigorating salty air of the ocean. Sometimes we visited the waterfront at the San Francisco marina, but most often we went to Ocean Beach, where I was eventually able to take slow walks and relish the soft sand beneath my bare feet. We sometimes ended up at the Beach Chalet for lunch.

It was there that my dear friend Lynn told me her news. Lynn had been a magazine editor for years and, now semi-retired, was enjoying her freelance writing career. She was also a world traveler, like me, and had been planning to go to Nepal, except now she was telling me she wasn't going anywhere.

"Ali, I found a lump in my breast," Lynn said. "I saw my doctor and figured I'd get the results when I got back from Asia. I had my bags packed, ready to go, and was downstairs waiting for the taxi when my doctor called. It's cancer."

It was overwhelming news. My own mother had just gone through this. Lynn was, in fact, old enough to be my mother, yet more vibrant than most people I knew. She was tall and lean and fit. We'd been on assignments together, hiking in Switzerland, kayaking and snorkeling in Hawaii, horseback riding the Ruby Mountains of Nevada. And, with her usual straightforwardness, she'd already gone ahead and arranged for a mastectomy. She'd even pulled a card table out of the basement to set up beside her sick bed for the same things I'd slowly accumulated on my nightstand: pills, water, magazines, TV remote, music. My life had been yanked out from under me so quickly, but my friend was going into it with eyes open. I couldn't bear the thought of her "preparing."

We took many walks on the beach that year, both of us on our own path to convalescence. Our friendship naturally deepened from sharing this awakening of our own vulnerabilities and mortality. I like to think that the waves that lapped at our feet carried our anxieties far out to be buried in the deepest depths of the sea.

Oddly, I envied her cancer-support meetings. The people in Lynn's group understood and helped one another. Although I greatly appreciated the encouragement of my friends, sometimes my suffering felt so solitary.

But not always. Most touching was the "Ali's alive!" party my friends threw on March 25, 2000, at the Cliff House restaurant overlooking Ocean Beach in San Francisco. The place was packed. My body was still heavily bandaged, but I managed to hide it all under my baggy clothes. It was my first real night out since the accident, and we toasted the fact that I was actually here to enjoy it. It was overwhelming to be in a room surrounded by so much love. Friends arrived from out of town and even from out of the country, people who's lives I felt I had barely touched. And to my surprise, there was a hidden agenda: I was presented with a generous check to help pay for the mounting medical costs, instigated by my friends Elliot and Jeff. Since it would be quite a while before I was able to work and earn any substantial income again, this was an amazing gift.

At the end of April 2000, four months after the accident, I was offered a low-key assignment at a spa resort in the British Virgin Islands.

"Please," I begged Dr. Roberts when I ran the idea past him. "Say that I can go." My arm was still bound in a burn sleeve, and I couldn't carry much equipment yet, but I was anxious to get back out in the world. And it was clear that I was making us both crazy.

"All right," he said, finally relenting. "But don't lift anything over ten pounds."

"And no scuba diving!" he yelled after me. But I was already gleefully racing down the hallway. Well, as fast as I could hobble with a cane anyway.

Once buckled into my seat on the plane, I began worrying how my lungs would hold up; this was my first flight since leaving Thailand. When we were kids, Andrew had drawn a series of comic books called *Alison's Black Cloud,* about bad things that seemed to follow me wherever I went, although he had graciously included a silver lining in the cloud because I always somehow seemed to emerge from these catastrophic events. The theme had followed me into adulthood and become a long-running joke among my friends—that no one should travel with me because there were too many near misses, too many scrapes with scattered death and destruction throughout my path in life.

Therefore I couldn't believe it when just as we leveled off the flight attendant who was leaning over to serve me breakfast suddenly keeled over in the aisle. Apparently he was having a heart attack. Luckily, there were cardiac defibrillators on the plane. We made an emergency landing in Las Vegas, and I watched the ambulances surrounding our plane. Hmmm, I thought, maybe now would be a good opportunity to jump off. But I didn't. I was fine. And thankfully so was the flight attendant. (I later called the airline to check on him.) Getting on a plane again had been an encouraging step. It was a short trip, just a few days, but the sun and ocean revived me. I wasn't exactly covering revolutions anymore, but it was a start.

Now that I felt more assured that I could fly, I went to Denver to visit my family. It was an emotional reunion with Andrew and his daughters, these important people to whom I'd written such heartfelt good-byes just a few months previously. It was the sweetest sound in the world to walk through the door and hear three-year-old Claire scream, "Aunt Ali!" I bent down and hugged her tightly (I wasn't strong enough to lift her yet), stroking her long strawberry blond hair. It had always been tradition that I'd return from my travels with gifts for the girls, and somehow the small, squeaky purple shoes I had bought for Claire had made it back with me from Thailand. They fit perfectly, and we were now able to hear her every step as she raced from room to room.

It was hard to believe that I was actually cradling the gentle-natured baby Hannah in my bandaged arms. She was the niece I was sure I would never meet. Hannah was the spitting image of a Gerber baby, and I basked in her cooing and the big blue eyes that were oblivious to the motivation she'd given me to be here right now.

My father, retired and still battling his own illness, was now living close to Andrew and his family and was at the house when I arrived. Dad and I, each with cane in hand, accompanied little Claire to the playground. We were amused at her boundless energy since neither of us had anything like the same vigor right then. My seventy-five-year-old father was now more mobile than I was, though his body was riddled with cancer. He sat stoically next to me, but his tearful eyes never left my face. Nothing more needed to be said. I appreciated how difficult it had been for my father to let his only daughter travel the world and to sit back and watch me take the risks I took over the years. But he had always encouraged me to believe that I could do anything and had given me the wings to fly.

Dad had endured years of my exploits from afar, and while Andrew and I had always tried to protect him from bad news, there was no hiding this.

"Watch me, watch me!" Claire yelled, completing what had to have been her tenth run down the slide. Dad and I sat on a bench watching, and I clapped each time at her accomplishment. I felt such joy at just being there.

Six months into my recovery I was invited to have a photo exhibit and give a talk about my Tibet work at the Smithsonian Institution. It was a childhood dream for me to give such a presentation, and I was determined to accept the invitation. It was my first public appearance after the accident, and organizing the photos and lecture boosted my confidence to work again. Unfortunately, on the way to Washington I developed another bout of blood poisoning from some glass that my arm wasn't able to spit out. As I dutifully took my prescribed antibiotics, Dr. Johnson insisted that I return home, warning me that what I was suffering could be potentially life threatening. I refused, and continued on, rallying to give my presentation at the Sackler Gallery.

I spoke passionately about the people in my images and their struggles for freedom in a country that I'd come to love.

"When I say I'm glad to be here, I really mean it," I told the audience. Later that day, I listened as Richard Gere got up to speak of his support for Tibet. When he led hundreds of us on a protest march from the National Mall to the Chinese embassy, I determinedly followed, despite my difficulty walking.

But I was a little too ambitious. Limping along, I pushed myself too hard and caused myself more serious injury. Once back in California, the doctor discovered that my toes had become dislocated because there were no longer muscles holding them together.

It was clear that this healing business was destined to become a long process. As I would recover from one ailment, the next would be waiting its turn to appear. Every step forward felt like it brought me ten steps back, and that's probably what pushed me to make my rash pronouncement.

"You certainly won't be able to continue traveling and working as a photographer," one of my specialists told me while addressing the problems I was having walking since my return from Washington. "You need to accept that this is who you are now." He suggested I reconsider what I was going to do with my life now that my former career and activities were beyond me. The gauntlet had been thrown down, and I rose to the challenge.

"I'm not only going to travel again," I replied, "I'm going to climb Mount Kilimanjaro for my fortieth birthday!"

It was an idea blurted out in total defiance, but I immediately latched on to it. My birthday was just over a year away, so I figured I'd have time to prepare. Kilimanjaro isn't a technical climb, but at 19,340 feet it's about 1,500 feet higher than the most difficult climb I'd made before, to the Everest Base Camp in Nepal. It would prove to the world and to myself that my heart, lungs, and body were back in working order.

That is, if I made it.

"I'm sending you to a psychiatrist!" another one of my doctors said when he heard about my grand plan. "You're in denial!" Kilimanjaro, after all, is the highest point in Africa—an ice-capped dormant volcano that sends about two-thirds of the people who attempt it back down with altitude sickness. Summiting it requires a five- or six-day trek, and on the last day you ascend a (literally) breathtaking four thousand feet.

But I wasn't in denial. The plan to climb Kilimanjaro gave me the focus I needed. Even saying it out loud made me feel euphoric. I knew what it was like to reach for that next moment in life and realize it might not be there. And with that came an awareness—I had never really appreciated my life until I almost died. With my newfound determination to make the climb, I finally felt I was discovering a sense of purpose.

Now I needed to get optimistic doctors on board and weed out the naysayers. Meeting Dr. Johnson and realizing that there actually were such good medical providers in the system, encouraged me to become more proactive, to take more control of my own healing and well-being. I changed doctors and physical therapists, finding supportive physicians who believed I could fully recover. At last, I felt that there was light at the end of this long dark tunnel. I had managed, in an incredibly complex and often infuriating health-care system, to find truly remarkable medical practitioners who genuinely cared and believed in me as a person. That was a huge a step.

"Tell me what I can do, not what I can't do," I pleaded with Susan Hobbel, my new physical therapist, as I stumbled through her door on crutches nearly seven months after the accident. "I want to go on a kayaking trip in Alaska next month. I can't walk properly yet, but I think I could maneuver a kayak. My goal is to climb Mount Kilimanjaro next year," I added. I waited for her to refer me to a shrink.

Susan unclipped the X-rays from the light box and looked me squarely in the eye. "We'll get you back out there doing the things you love," she said, "but you have to be patient with the healing process. No kayaking yet." She was firm, but I felt that I had finally found an ally.

Susan was about my age, and I think she related to the fact that I wasn't simply trying to get back to a desk job. She was a hugely motivating physical therapist and just what I needed. I met with her at least twice a week, and during each session she challenged me, sometimes to the point of tears.

We quickly developed a symbiotic relationship. Whereas my initial goals were admittedly lofty—kayaking and summiting mountains—she recognized my significant limitations. We first had to concentrate on getting all four of my limbs functioning again before I could even think about exercise as I knew it. We did a lot of one-on-one, hands-on, very simple exercises at first, just moving my foot in a circle or lifting it off the bed. I couldn't believe how many months of work it took just to get some muscle coordination back. There were times when I would hit flat spots, and we had to push through physical and mental barriers as I worked through the fear of carrying on despite the obvious pain. What made the experience so synergistic was that Susan saw how motivated I was and she was not afraid herself to push me to my limits. She also worked closely with my trainer and eventually crafted a regimen for me at my local gym—the same place where I'd been an aerobics fanatic in what was now my previous life.

Time may be a great healer, but developing patience became my greatest challenge. Even with the full arsenal of American health care available to me, my recuperation time seemed glacially slow. I'd always been athletic, and it was that storehouse of health that helped me survive the initial trauma of the bus collision and its aftermath. But it could only take me so far.

In the past I'd thrived on jogging, kayaking, hiking, skiing, scuba diving, and yoga. Now, lifting a two-pound weight was a challenge. But I refused to give up. When one doctor told me that due to all the surgeries I'd never have abdominal muscles again, I started doing as many sit-ups as I could. Slowly, I worked up to more than a thousand a day. Within the year I was eventually able to work out slowly on elliptical machines to develop my lower body strength and my heart and lungs.

Despite all this effort, my EKGs were abnormal, which meant that I'd had serious heart trauma. My doctor described it as a "bruised peach." Even though it had been damaged, I figured that since it's a muscle, it too could be developed. I knew that my bar was higher than most, and although I would have to redefine my idea of "normal," I wanted to see what I was capable of. It made me even more determined to get out and do as much as I possibly could with this fabulous life that I'd regained. "If not now, when?"

Of course, I did have my dark moments, grappling with the immense discomfort and frustration of my slow healing process. After all, it was more than two years before I could walk properly again and many more before I could manage without pain. I struggled with bouts of self-doubt. Was I making things worse by pushing myself so hard? Was it time to accept that the damage to my body was irreversible and start a new and different life? But when those thoughts arose, I would remember what I'd learned about courage while on that dirt floor in Laos, and my doubts would recede before a more powerful belief: whatever the future brought, I could get through it.

CHAPTER 15

If I was going to make it to Africa, I wanted to test my capabilities first with more challenging travels. In September 2000, nine months after the accident, I got a call from Cathy Tedford, the curator of a small gallery in upstate New York, who handled the traveling exhibitions of my photographs.

It was great to hear her voice. I had met Cathy a couple of years before, when she'd had an exhibition of my Tibet photos. The event revolved around a demonstration of Tibetan dancers, thangka painters, and monks making sand *mandalas*. Cathy didn't just produce exhibitions, she created events. She told me that she'd just gotten some funding for an upcoming show she was organizing on Inuit art. Her idea was to purchase some of their sculptures and lithographs to display in the gallery. She wanted to know if I would be interested in documenting the featured Inuit artists and their way of life, and showing my photographs along with their artwork. "How are you feeling?" she asked. "Are you up for going to the Arctic?"

I didn't even hesitate. Within weeks we headed to Nunavut in the Canadian Arctic. I was still limping, and the cold intensified the irritation in my joints, forcing me to bundle up in many layers while laden with camera gear. But I was thrilled to be reviving my adventurous lifestyle after so many months of intermittent bed rest. Cathy and I stayed in local guesthouses, usually someone's converted home, or old fishing lodges. I photographed the hunters as they sought out whales and seals on their hunting trips. I gleaned valuable insights into their culture, such as: if you pee you'll stay warmer in the cold outdoors, because of an empty bladder, and that there is no point in playing dead with a polar bear because no matter what you do you will have your brains scooped out and eaten within a few minutes anyway. It felt good to be thinking about things like that again.

With the demise of the sale of skins and fur, the Inuit economy had been slowly plummeting to a subsistence level. Once a self-sufficient culture, many Inuit have since become reliant on processed food and food stamps. There are few jobs in a land covered with snow and ice for most of the year.

Recently, a few Inuit have become successful through the sales of traditional art. Initially encouraged by a young Canadian artist named James Houston, who set up a shop in Cape Dorset in the 1950s, the local artisans were taught how to make lithographic prints and to market the figures they sculpted from locally processed soapstone. The success behind this project lay in the fact that instead of selling these original polar bear and seal sculptures as crafts, Houston put high prices on them and editioned the lithographs so they were valued as art.

Consequently, Inuit art is now a thriving business, and on this particular trip I traveled to the Canadian Eastern Arctic from Baffin Island to Cape Dorset and Pangnirtung to photograph some of the better-known artists. It was on the island of Pangnirtung that I was invited to a picnic, a recreational activity I found difficult to imagine enjoying in subzero temperatures. I waddled up to the beach in my multiple layers of fleece to find everyone else bundled up in so much fur it was difficult to distinguish them from what we were about to eat.

And that, I quickly discovered, was the rub. On the table were a number of large frozen caribou: bodies, heads, and appendages being cleanly sliced with *ulos*, the local rounded knives. A woman handed me a pair of eyebrows, small fuzzy brown slivers that reminded me of the caterpillars I used to collect as a kid. I hesitated. "Here you go," she insisted cheerily. Not wanting to seem culturally insensitive, I took them into the palm of my hand with feigned enthusiasm. In a moment of panic I surreptitiously slipped the caribou eyebrows into my Gore-Tex jacket pocket.

Two young girls broke through the blizzarding snow, licking heartily at their soft-serve ice cream cones. "Good Lord," I thought, "this is a hardy bunch."

Our main meal was in fact two nice fat seals, which had just been pulled up wet and fresh from the salty water. With a grunt the men slit them open, the warm steam erupting from their bloated bellies. One of the men shoveled some of the raw intestines onto my plate. And then he offered the eyeballs. "They have a texture like grapes," the young man scooping them from the seal head assured me. As much as I appreciated their generosity I simply couldn't bring myself to eat seal sushi. That too quickly went into my pocket.

It was then that I noticed the dogs. Although, I should point out, they noticed me first. One, then two, then a pack surrounded me, smelling the aroma of fresh meat wafting around me. My fear of dogs was now surpassed by my dread of being caught by my hosts, who were probably wondering why I was being followed by every canine in town. At first I walked away casually, back in the direction from which I'd come, hoping to escape unnoticed. But aggressive huskies now snapped at my legs, their teeth gnashing at my blue jacket. I began to run while tossing animal parts back toward the pack, pursued in a sharklike feeding frenzy. I prayed I wouldn't encounter any polar bears along the way.

I felt an affinity for the people of Iqaluit just by reading the handwritten entrepreneurial notes and job requests pinned on the wall of the local supermarket. These people lived in million-dollar homes, and not because they were mansions. It costs thousands of dollars to embed every single pylon holding up each house with a special drill into the ever-shifting permafrost of the tundra. Food was frightfully expensive. Jobs were scarce.

Most of the messages tacked to the wall were double barreled:

"Four-wheel jeep for sale. Mechanic for hire."

"Babysitter, housecleaner, or just plain company available."

"Slightly broken coffee maker for sale. Filter basket missing, pot cracked."

"Earn some extra money. Learn how to make sealskin gloves while in your own home."

I was daydreaming about what it would be like to rent a bungalow, buy a Land Rover, apply for a waitressing job, and move up here to the Arctic when Zinour's listing caught my eye: "Massage available. Experienced masseuse can work out painful muscles. Paintings also for sale."

I had been desperately missing my team of bodywork specialists. Maybe a massage would help. Shooting photos was still a challenge; I continued to have occasional numbness in my arm from my back injury. A number of times I'd be focusing on a subject when my fingers froze up and the camera slipped from my grip. I always had to make sure to keep the strap around my neck.

And that's how I met Zinour, a striking Inuit with long dark hair, and his spunky blonde wife, Gail, and their two boys, who among many things taught me the best way to cut the claws off a seal. They lived within walking distance of my guesthouse, and I was often invited to eat dinner with them.

Gail eventually asked if I would mind making a meal for them one night. "We really want to try a typical California dinner."

I briefly entertained the idea of tacos, until I discovered nothing in the market that even resembled avocados, taco shells, or salsa. I decided on Arctic char, a delicious local fish similar to a flaky salmon; it seemed like something even I could cook. So maybe it wasn't Californian, but I decided they might really appreciate it if I caught it myself. Despite the fact that I'd only been ocean fishing twice in my life, I bought a license and lined up a boat to take me out the next morning. When I got to the shore, the seas were so rough, and the warnings so severe, I opted not to go. The fishermen who owned the boat went anyway and, as it turned out, went missing for three days, bobbing in the Arctic seas, wearing only shorts and with nothing to drink but whiskey.

Instead I opted to buy a fish, but it was frozen solid from top to bottom. I hadn't counted on that. I needed to defrost this thing fast, before Gail and Zinour got home. When I got to their house I filled up the bathtub with scalding hot water and dropped the fish into it. I leaned over the tub a half hour later to find a mass of flaky scum floating on the water. But it was less the now-unrecognizable fish that stopped me in my tracks than the undeniable spasms that were shooting from my abdomen. I lifted my shirt. And there, in the dim light of the bathroom mirror, peeking through the railroad-track stitches lining my stomach was a large lump that looked distinctly like my intestines were trying to break out through my gut. During my initial surgery in Thailand I had been sewn back together from my chest to my pelvis, and now it looked as though the stitches were separating. I was literally ripping apart at the seams. I had a flash of the beached seals with their carved open bellies.

Distractedly, I scooped the mess into a cooking pan, where I reshaped it into the form of a fish, placing the delectable eyeballs where I imagined they should go, and popped the whole thing in the oven. "Wow, it smells great in here," Gail exclaimed when she walked through the door an hour later.

The meal was greeted with a cross between camouflaged shock (the parents) and outright screams of revulsion (the kids). "Mom, what is that?!" cried Greisha, Gail and Zinour's eldest son. "Please don't make us eat it!" Gail got up and saved the day by making fish soup. I was never asked to cook again.

Although there was something definitely very wrong with me, it never occurred to me to leave and go home. When I rejoined Cathy, we flew from Cape Dorset to Baffin Island. "I hate flying," Cathy announced as we each found window seats.

"Yeah, well, I hate giving birth to my entrails," I thought as I rubbed my expanding stomach. "Ugh, why is my body constantly trying to sabotage me?"

Cathy popped a pill and promptly fell asleep, which was a good thing because halfway through the flight an Inuit woman called out to the pilots with surprising composure, "Excuse me, but there seems to be a small fire in the aisle." Sure enough, dense black smoke was filling the cabin. The copilot did a double take and reached behind his seat to an empty bracket that I guessed had once held a fire extinguisher.

"Oh jeez, the landing gear's caught fire!" the copilot yelled to the pilot, something I had never really wanted to hear at thirty thousand feet.

"You're frigging kidding me," I thought to myself. Was there really a little black cloud following me around? No, I realized, it was smoke.

Sputtering, the passengers began fanning the fumes. No oxygen masks were dropping from the ceiling on this flight. I began gasping for air through the neck warmer I had pulled over my mouth. I looked across the aisle at the woman who had first noticed the fire. She was cradling an infant in her arms and put a shirt over the baby's face to help it breathe. Oh my God, she's got a kid.

"Please put on the orange life jackets, which you'll find under the seats," the copilot announced. This didn't instill much confidence as I eyed the pristine blue icebergs bobbing along below us. I figured we had about thirty seconds in that water before hypothermia would set in.

"Tuck and brace, everyone, we're making an emergency descent," yelled the pilot, "and I have no idea if our landing gear is working!" I looked out the window and was relieved to see that at least we'd made it to the airport. Dozens of fire trucks, police cars, and ambulances were lined up on the tarmac.

"Is this finally it?" I thought as I tucked my head into my lap and grabbed my knees as instructed. My life had been a string of near misses. "Did I live through that bus accident just to die in this plane crash?" Surprisingly, I felt incredibly calm. Had I really accomplished anything in these last ten months? Didn't I go through all that hard work to come back and do more with my life?

"Hold on!" yelled the pilot. When I peeked through the windows I could see green trees whizzing past. There was a heavy thud as we made contact with the ground, then the scraping of metal as we bumped and slid down the runway. We fishtailed back and forth like a pachinko ball. And then, amazingly, we stopped.

Everyone cheered. The doors immediately flew open, and we hungrily gulped the fresh air. Firefighters rushed on board, giving oxygen to the baby and others who needed it. I waved them away and walked off. Cathy woke up with a little snort. "That's why I hate these small planes," she complained as she rubbed the medicated sleep from her eyes. "These landings are always so bumpy."

So I'd survived a crash landing and avoided three days missing on the seas, but now I had to deal with this unsightly protuberance appearing through my abdomen.

I went to the hospital as soon as I returned to San Francisco. In addition to my tearing stitches I was concerned that I was still having so much difficulty with my foot and legs, and that I still sometimes lost feeling and mobility in my arms. Before I went away, I had been put back on Neurontin, my nerve medication, and received electric-shock treatments in my appendages to see if that helped stimulate feeling. Also, sounds had become disturbingly muffled and tests showed that I had lost partial hearing from the impact. It seemed there was always something waiting to take the front seat.

As Dr. Roberts reviewed my new charts his impatience was apparent. "Listen, stop requesting all these tests. You have to accept that you are not the person you were; you never will be. The bus took that away from you."

I was incensed. Even Dr. Roberts was losing faith in me. Why was everyone telling me I just had to accept that this is who I am? I didn't accept it. I refused to acknowledge that I would never get my life back, no matter what anybody said. Was no one on my side? I had once been so strong and felt I could do anything. It seemed that all I kept hearing was what I couldn't do, what I would never do again.

Dr. Roberts pointed to the notebook that I was scribbling my notes into. "Okay, you have time for one more question and then I have to go."

"Well, what is this bulge in my stomach?" I asked. "It looks like my guts are poking through it." With a quick prod to my belly he confirmed it was exactly that; the scar tissue was tearing from the previous surgery.

"You need to have your intestines pushed back in and your abdomen sewn up and repaired. It's a major operation." I was mortified. Not only at what was happening to my body, but at his asperity. I had used up my one final question, and without further comment he abruptly left, shutting the door behind him.

Once again I changed doctors. I didn't have room in my life for negativity. I needed to surround myself with a confident support team of doctors, physical therapists, chiropractor, trainer, and bodywork specialists because sometimes my own frustrations ran deep: whenever I made some progress, I'd have to have another operation. They needed to believe, as I did, that in just over a year, on my birthday, I would reach my goal: standing on top of that snow-covered peak of Kilimanjaro.

On Halloween night, October 31, 2000, I was admitted into the hospital for a ventral hernia operation. My intestines would be rearranged and my abdomen reinforced with plastic mesh to keep my organs in place.

We were hours behind schedule when the heavyset doctor returned to the foot of my bed and told me he had a couple more surgeries to perform. Did I want to wait or to come back tomorrow? He sounded exhausted, so despite the fact that I was already hooked up to an IV and ready to be wheeled in, I opted to leave. I was reminded not to eat for another twenty-four hours. It was unsettling to wind through the San Francisco streets in that woozy state of mind, dancing witches and ghosts emerging from the dark Halloween night, pressing their grinning faces against the window of my car.

I came back the next morning and went through the whole

prepping procedure again. Now I was really nervous, and I started having some serious flashbacks. The nurse gave me a shot of Demerol to calm my nerves, and I put on my CD player headphones. I counted as instructed: ninety-nine, ninety-eight, ninety-seven, ninety-six, ninety-five . . .

It was three days before I could even lift my head.

"I couldn't believe how much anesthesia we had to give you to knock you out," the anesthesiologist told me when I was finally able to acknowledge his existence. He added that it was pretty normal considering all the other surgeries I'd had and the drugs I'd been on. "But we were concerned when your blood pressure plummeted."

I was overwhelmed with the feeling that something dreadful had happened during the surgery. I had a distinct mental image that I'd had an out-of-body experience, that I was hovering above myself looking down at my body on the operating table, surrounded by machines and frantic doctors.

"It didn't go well, did it? I feel like I died. Did you bring me back?" I asked Dr. Lubowsky, my surgeon, when he stopped in to see me on his rounds.

"No, of course not," he assured me. My belief that something traumatic had happened was so profound I thought maybe he was covering it up. I even asked the nurses and attending intern, who had been in the room, but everyone confidently relayed the same answer. All had gone smoothly.

I was hospitalized for a week and bedridden for five. After so many surgeries the buildup of anesthesia in my system meant that I was racked with nausea. But this time it wasn't going away, and we couldn't figure out why. The surgeon insisted it was in my mind. He obviously didn't know me.

Much to the annoyance of Dr. Lubowsky, I persisted. I had ultrasounds and insisted on other opinions. It turned out a raging infection had set in, and I was put on antibiotics. I felt vindicated, although it took months to recover from this, yet another setback.

I had barely regained my health again when in March 2001 I finally agreed to have foot surgery. The doctor had discovered a tumor in my foot that was contributing to making walking so agonizing. Susan, my physical therapist, teased me because I lived in my high-top basketball sneakers, but I simply couldn't find any comfortable shoes. I had tried acupuncture, bodywork, and endured nine months of cortisone shots being administered directly into my feet, but finally saw no other option than to have the operation.

Foot surgery set me back yet again. I was laid up for another month. Slowly, first with crutches and later with a cane, I forced myself to walk to and from the hospital for my therapy sessions—two torturous miles each way. Focusing on small goals like this gave me the power to go on, avoiding the chasm of fear always ready to suck me into its deep abyss.

I was thrilled when I finally didn't have to wear the compression sleeve on my arm anymore but shocked at how often people stopped me in public to ask how I'd gotten so badly burned or where I had been attacked by a shark or bear. It always took me by surprise because I was so busy trying to get well that I didn't think about how I looked. To avoid the remarks, it would be years before I wore short sleeves again.

But in other ways life was getting back to normal. Eventually, I even started to date again.

"I admire you for everything you've gone through," the first man I was intimate with told me before hesitating, "but I just can't get past the scars."

When he said that, I immediately remembered a time I was walking through a Tibetan carpet factory in Nepal, bantering with the women as they looped their yarn through the big wooden looms.

"Do you have children?" a young woman asked while engaged in making an intricately patterned carpet. It was a typical question.

"No."

She looked up from her weaving in surprise. "Are you married?"

"No."

Her hands had now stopped in midair. "Why?" she asked in sincere puzzlement. "Are you ugly?"

It had been refreshing to live in a culture that was not consumed with Western ideas of beauty and our exhausting notions of perfection. Until my own disfigurement, I had no idea how painfully judgmental people can actually be, simply on the basis of looking different. No wonder every doctor had mentioned how lucky I was that nothing had happened to my face. I saw now what they meant.

These scars became a badge of courage. I owned them. I turned to my date. "Well, the scars aren't going anywhere, but you are." And I slammed the door behind him.

It was a devastating reentry to romantic life.

I never lost sight of my goal to summit Mount Kilimanjaro for my birthday, and it continued to motivate my recovery. Eventually, I was able again to prepare for the climb. The following year was a haze of doctors' visits and physical therapy. My biggest adjustment was learning to measure my physical progress in much smaller increments than before the accident. Yoga became an integral part of my life. My yoga practice helped me enormously, not only in reclaiming my flexibility, but also in creating a respect and a newfound awareness of the compromised body I now had to adjust to. At times I felt so defeated that I'd dissolve into tears. But as I progressed, I came to think my tears were not just from frustration—they seemed to be releasing the pain and fear buried so deep in me. Instead of getting angry at its limitations, I now allowed myself to marvel at my body's healing capacity.

I was thrilled that I had accomplished something as adventurous as traveling to the Arctic, but after numerous impediments I was ready to attempt a more physically challenging trip. It was a year later than when I had initially proposed the idea to Susan, my physical therapist, but in July 2001, about one and a half years after the accident, I finally got to fulfill my ambition to kayak in Alaska. Paddling among the magnificent sapphire blue icebergs in the quiet of Frederick Sound and Glacier Bay, I listened for the throaty eruption of the friendly humpback whales as they'd emerge from the ocean a few feet from the kayaks. Rafts of sea otters floated by on their backs, followed by pods of orcas diving alongside us.

"It just doesn't get better than this," I said to my guide as we sat in our beach chairs watching the last alpine glow of the pink sunset spread across the still water one evening. There was a distinct rainbow arching in the distance. "Life is good." I found myself saying that a lot now.

That night, as I lay in my tent, I felt a wave of appreciation—to be immersed back in nature and the outdoor life I thrived on—while sleeping under a canopy of stars. Bathed in their twinkling glow, they seemed to beckon me, peeking through my tent flap. Wherever I've gone around the world the stars have been the one constant. They'd watched over me when I'd felt alone in the outback of Australia, was afraid in Laos, and awe inspired in Tibet. And what about Mount Kailash—would I ever see them blanket the roof of the world in Tibet again, that country that I loved so much? Would they follow me to Africa? Falling asleep, I took refuge in their gaze as they winked and blinked from the blackness, steady with their infinite abundance of assurance.

186

CHAPTER 16

The Alaska trip strengthened my resolve by reassuring me that I would be up for the physical challenge of climbing Kilimanjaro. Although I had numerous painful laser surgeries on my arm during the next six months, my legs got stronger and I was finally able to walk without my "sticks," as a boy in the British Virgin Islands had called them. I was traveling again; I worked out at the gym nearly every day; and in the fall of 2001 I managed a slow jog of three miles on the beach in San Francisco. My first run! I was so delighted I ran right up to a startled Vietnamese fisherman and hugged him, right there on the beach.

Even so, I was concerned about the excessive damage to my lungs and heart and continued to meet with an extensive array of doctors to prepare for my Africa trip. Not only did I want to make sure that my lungs would survive in the 19,340-foot altitude, but

I also wanted to find out if they would hold up in deep pressure under the sea. I wanted to know if it was safe for me to scuba dive again, and I consulted Dr. Cianci, a top dive and hyperbaric medicine specialist. I was surprised, when I left his waiting room, to see so many women breast cancer survivors filling the hyperbaric chambers in the adjacent hospital room. As he ushered me into his office, Dr. Cianci explained how the pressure helps relieve their irritation from radiation.

I told him my plans to climb the mountain and that, as an experienced scuba diver, I hoped to dive again. "If it's something I can't do anymore, I'll accept that, but if I can, I'd certainly like to continue doing it," I told him.

Dr. Cianci explained that climbing a mountain is actually less of a risk than diving, which is a much more abrupt change in altitude. I was surprised when he told me that it is the first ten feet of diving that causes the most increased pressure. "There's no way to quantify the extent of scar tissue or other damage to your lungs, which means they could explode or have trouble expanding. If you were my daughter, I wouldn't allow it; it's too risky." He looked at me, and I'm sure he could see my disappointment. "But if you were my daughter, you would insist on going anyway. Although," he added cautiously, "you would have to promise to be very careful."

Driving home from Dr. Cianci's office I mulled over something else he had said after my lengthy physical and reviewing my chart.

"I don't know if you were a spiritual person before," he said, "but I hope you are now." He told me that he had been a surgeon in Vietnam for years, and had never seen anyone survive injuries the extent of mine. "From a medical standpoint, you should absolutely not be here right now. I want you to think about that every day for the rest of your life."

I had heard this sentiment from many of my doctors. It was a moving reminder of how close I had come, and always gave me pause. Yet, in some ways I felt pressured by it. Was I worthy of living up this? I felt that maybe I should be dedicating my life to working at Mother Teresa's, not performing such insignificant acts as washing my car. I was determined to continue living my life to its fullest, yet now I had an even greater appreciation of the seemingly small things along the way.

It was difficult to feel the ordinariness of everyday life after surrendering to death. I was determined to stay in touch with my hard-won sense of its sacredness. Sometimes I had to let the preciousness go a bit, just to function and get through the day, and it saddened me to feel it slipping away. Yet, as life drew me back into its busy whirl, my meditation practice or even just stopping to take a breath and bring awareness to the moment helped me to return to the touchstone that was that sacred place. It was as if I'd taken my hand and wiped at the steamy pane of glass I'd been looking through. It was starting to clear.

Later that month I was invited to be on a television special for people who had experienced near-death scenarios. I struggled with finding the right words and felt that my story was still too emotionally raw to be compressed into sound bites. At one point a woman stood up and exclaimed her disbelief that each one of us had experienced an overall feeling of love while being encompassed by a white light at our time of "death." "When you're dyin' there ain't no white light," she announced. "It's just those endorphins kicking in."

"Sister," I thought, "if I can lie broken and dying alone on some roadside in Laos and feel unafraid and okay about it, I don't care what it is." But I knew in my heart it was something much bigger than that. It was, in fact, a life force much bigger than all of us.

CHAPTER 17

It was December 2001—almost two years after the accident and just weeks before my fortieth birthday—and there I was, finally arriving in East Africa. I was still in chronic pain, but mentally I felt up to the challenge of climbing Mount Kilimanjaro. First I needed to acclimatize to the area and culture. I was also working again on my photography book about children, which had been put on hold during my recovery. I was determined to see its completion.

I first traveled in Kenya, on my own, with a driver. John was terrific company, a seven-foot-two Masai accompanying me, a five-foot-two blonde. In the town of Nakuru, he dropped me at a local guesthouse, warning me to go straight to my room while he parked the car. When he came in a few minutes later, John found me in the packed and raucous bar, having a drink with the locals.

"You don't know fear, do you?" he asked, looking around in apparent discomfort as he took a seat next to me.

"Why? Should I?" I asked, honestly surprised. He just shook his head and laughed as I called the waiter over for a couple of beers

I wasn't sure how the Masai would react to a white woman pulling up in a Land Rover and pitching a tent in the middle of the Masai Mara on her own except for her driver, but I figured I had been accepted when the headman from the closest community came to visit and presented me with a ball of fur the size of a softball. He informed me that it was a hair ball a lion had coughed up. His wife then followed with a warthog tusk, and I was invited back to take photographs in their village. In the following days, I had a continuous group of Masai *moran,* or warriors, lined up outside my tent, wanting to be photographed and to take turns holding up the large light reflectors.

Around the Shaba National Reserve there is some tribal conflict because the Samburu and Masai still raid each other's cattle, so the guards were adamant that I hire a couple of soldiers to escort me. Dressed in full camouflage and brandishing automatic weapons, they attempted to impress me with stories of bandits they had shot. I left one soldier to guard my tent while another accompanied me during the day in the four-wheel drive. The Samburu warriors in the surrounding area performed their jumping mating dances, and the women sang deep from their throats. They wore bright, boldly printed dresses, ornate beaded jewelry, and elaborate headgear. The men had freshly decorated faces with flowers and feathers protruding from their heads. With exquisite straight-backed posture, the young men gracefully jumped high in the air as an expression of their attraction and an attempt to engage the young women who watched. In the evening, one of the pregnant women in the village began to go into labor and asked me and my driver to bring her to the hospital in town, which was over an hour away. She held her belly and screamed in anguish from the front seat while her husband and the soldier with his AK-47 were squeezed into the back. The rifle would bang the roof every time we hit one of the numerous potholes. The woman gave birth to a healthy girl and was so grateful that she named her baby after me. The first Alison Samburu, I'm sure.

I eventually flew to Tanzania. Beneath the shadow of Longido Mountain, outside of Arusha, where I would soon begin my ascent of Kilimanjaro, I set up my small nylon tent beside a Masai community. The holes in the ears of the warriors were so big that they carried their snuff bottles in the elongated loops. That evening, the Masai taught me how they roast goat on a stick over the open fire. I reciprocated by cooking bread on a stick—toast. I showed them photos of my family, and they introduced me to theirs. They stumped me with questions like, "How big are oceans? What do they look like? What does snow feel like? What is cold?"

The next morning the men asked if I wanted to go to the market. A barrage of painted warriors piled into the Land Rover, spears sticking through the sunroof. Just when I thought one more couldn't possibly fit, another would squeeze into the backseat or onto the top of the truck. I simply couldn't believe it when they stopped for an old man with a plow and he pulled it onto the hood of the car with ropes. Driving along, I saw my first wild animal in Tanzania, a giraffe. I excitedly jumped out to take a picture. To the Masai, seeing a giraffe in the wild is like seeing a squirrel in New Jersey, and their incessant laughter upon my return dispelled any worries I had conjured up about being intimidated by these fierce warriors.

At last it was time for the climb. The permit alone to summit Kilimanjaro costs about six hundred dollars, so to help cut costs, while in the States, I had found a local Tanzania-based company, on the Internet, to get me up the mountain. I had received a number of e-mails supporting their services. In Arusha I organized a meeting with yet another John, the company owner, to discuss the equipment he would provide. I reluctantly handed over most of my traveler's checks to cover the permit, food, and a guide. Then I went into an Internet café to check my e-mail while he went to buy supplies.

I was surprised to open a message that read: "I cracked this guy's e-mail account and found that you two have been corresponding. WHATEVER YOU DO—DON'T GIVE HIM YOUR MONEY! He's a crook. He has just gotten out of jail and is working under a false name. He'll tell you his name is John but his real name is

Wailu. We paid him to do a trek, but he took our money and we never saw him again. He's done the same to others. He doesn't even have a license to climb Kilimanjaro . . . All those e-mails you think you have been receiving from other travelers touting his services are actually from him." I couldn't believe the timing. The e-mailer went on to say that because he had been ripped off he was now contacting everyone he could to warn them.

My jaw dropped. I had just handed this alleged thief a good portion of my savings. I bolted out the door and ran down the street.

There he was! "Hey, Wailu," I yelled out his other name. When he looked up I knew the e-mailer was right. John/Wailu had no intention of organizing my trek. I quickly snapped his picture.

Then I grabbed him by the collar. I was furious. I had been visualizing climbing this mountain for nearly two years, not to mention painstakingly saving my money. "I know who you are!" I yelled. "Don't even think of screwing me over, or I'll report you to the police right now and get you thrown back in jail! You have no idea what I went through to get here!" He started to protest, but it was obvious I was onto him.

He refused to return my money, but I didn't leave his side until he found a reliable guide who agreed to get me up the mountain.

"Can we wait a few days and get some more people?" John/Wailu asked.

"No!" I had my sights set on being on top of that mountain for my birthday, and I wasn't giving up that dream now.

"Summit day December twenty-third," I insisted. "Or I go with your photo to the police."

The next day I not only had my guide and food but I was presented with a fluffy new pink pillow for the excursion.

I was more than ready. My guide, Arusha (he was named after the town), planned to lead me up Kilimanjaro's Machame Route, which runs through rain forests, valleys, and over craggy plateaus, to Uhuru Peak, the mountain's summit. Climbing this snow-capped volcano on the equator would be like trekking from the Amazon to the Antarctic. I was a little worried about keeping up with the two others who had managed to join us on short notice: Kylie from Australia and Matt from Washington DC. For a start, they were both only eighteen years old. As for me, well, I would be going up the mountain at thirty-nine and coming down at forty.

By this time, I'd gone six months without using a cane, and my legs felt strong and fit, but the climb would be a challenge for my scarred lungs and weakened heart—not to mention my back. I used hiking poles for support as we hiked for five hours the first day, taking a gentle path through a green canopy of ferns, moss, and creepers. I was glad for my rain jacket as moisture fell from the trees through the muggy air. Locals passed us, barely breaking a sweat, carrying large loads of wood balanced gracefully on their heads. We were filthy and caked in mud as we set up camp at ninety-five hundred feet that night.

On the second day, it was another relatively easy tramp to twelve thousand feet despite the pounding rain. We were now in tropical terrain surrounded by otherworldly prehistoric-looking foliage. We passed plants that looked like something out of a Dr. Seuss book: senecios that resembled candelabras with pom-poms on top; red-hot poker flowers; and *Lobelia deckenii,* small green shrubs that closed up to protect themselves during the chilly nights but opened to the warm sun during the day.

At the Shira Plateau, the campsite was filled with dozens of travelers. That night I met five climbers from Colorado, playing Hacky Sack, who had read the story I had published in *Outside,* an adventure travel magazine, about the Laos bus crash. I had told two million readers my story, ending with the fact that I would be climbing Mount Kilimanjaro for my upcoming birthday. I knew then I couldn't back out. It was in writing.

But on day three, the cakewalk was over. The terrain changed to a sparse black lava-rock moonscape. My head pounded from the altitude, my hips ached, and stabs of soreness shot through my lower back. "I paid money for this?" I joked to Arusha. I knew the trek was only going to get tougher: the next two days were steep climbs into what would surely feel like the stratosphere. We camped a little lower than the previous night at Barranco Camp, eleven thousand feet.

News of my story and summit bid spread, and soon people were stopping me all the way up the mountain to give me high fives and shouts of support.

"Hey, we're rooting for you. We'll carry you up if we have to!" one couple told me.

"We'll be singing 'Happy Birthday' to you on the twenty-third," someone else called out in passing.

I never felt alone in my challenge. And that helped immensely.

On day four all I could do was plod, one agonizing step at a time. We made camp at 15,180 feet; I could hardly tear myself away from the sight of the dazzling snow-covered mountain glistening in the moonlight. But I also felt deep pangs of doubt. In a few hours I'd find out the truth about myself. Did I really have the stamina to make it?

It's difficult enough to do anything with a lack of food and sleep, but climbing four thousand feet is especially taxing. In order to reach the top by sunrise, we began climbing at midnight, following the tangerine moon. I was nauseated. My brain felt like it was cooking. The icy air pierced my scarred lungs, and breathing was agony. In desperation, I sucked glucose tablets, hoping they'd give me an energy boost.

"*Pole, pole,*" Arusha encouraged me in Swahili. "Slowly, slowly." I shot him a glance and laughed: What, did he think I was going to sprint? Up until now, I had carried all thirty or so pounds of my photo equipment, but the cold magnified the pain in my back, and I gratefully started handing it over, lens by lens, for Arusha to carry.

"Just breathe and climb," he muttered over and over. Not easy, as there was half as much oxygen here than at sea level. Still, I appreciated his words of support.

The path became a wall of crumbling scree, illuminated only by my headlamp. I briefly switched it off and looked up. Yes, the stars had followed me. I focused on my labored breath and thought back to my struggle to breathe in Laos, which reminded me of why I was doing this. I wasn't going to come this far and let the mountain beat me. Arusha motioned for me to stop and rest, but I shook my head. If I stopped now, I'd never start again.

And then, suddenly, Uhuru was in front of me. I had made it from the bananas to the pines to the ice. The sun began to rise, turning the glaciers pink and blue just as I reached the summit, the snows of Kilimanjaro. My eyes teared. Juha, a Finnish man I'd met on the trail, ran up and presented me with a hand-carved wooden cup as a trophy. "Congratulations!" he cried. "You made it! Happy birthday!"

On a whim, I dialed my friend Lynn's number in San Francisco on my cell phone. Our birthdays are a day apart, and every year she always celebrated with a combined Christmas party at her home. At first I got her machine, so I tried again and was surprised at the clarity of the connection.

"Hey, it's Ali," I yelled to her. "I'm on top of Kilimanjaro!" Her party was in full swing, and my friends thousands of miles away toasted me with champagne as the snow and wind whipped

199

my face. I had been at the same party the year before, leaning on crutches and vowing to everyone, "Next year, I'll be on top of the mountain." And there I was. "What can be better than to reach your goal and to share it with friends?" I thought.

Hannah and Claire, my young nieces, had painted their names on rocks, which I carried up and with a loving kiss placed in their new home. Now whenever the girls see pictures they know that their rocks are sitting on top of that mountain of greatness for eternity. With great difficulty I read the cards that Andrew had sent along, insisting I open them at the summit. The girls had drawn pictures of me waving from the pinnacle of Kilimanjaro, surrounded by giraffes, lions, and zebras.

Just as poignant were the words on Andrew's card: "I know I am supposed to write some words of inspiration, but it is hard to when you are the one who inspires me. All you have done and all you have seen—you have lived the lives of a thousand people. You have achieved, succeeded, surpassed, overcome, and conquered, all with compassion and a sense of humor. I am so proud to be your younger brother. I believe in you and I am inspired by you. Raise your arms up and celebrate, for today is your birthday!"

And that is exactly what I did.

A soft blanket of pink fog swirled below, and I felt as if I'd risen to the heavens. I stood on the precipice gulping air, awestruck, while relishing the moment of my accomplishment. I thought of the words that I now held so close to my heart, "Life is not measured by the number of breaths we take, but by the moments that take our breath away." I was certainly appreciating each and every one. A rim of crimson globe broke through the clouds. It was the dawning of a new day, a new decade for me—and, I realized, a new life.

PART III

eventually, you have to come down from the mountain

You gain strength, courage, and confidence by every experience in which you really stop to look fear in the face. You must do the thing which you think you cannot do.

—ELEANOR ROOSEVELT

CHAPTER 18

I had made it to the top of the mountain. Now, what about the bottom of the sea? It was a quiet day on the island of Zanzibar in Tanzania. Everyone was still recovering from the New Year's festivities. The sun was already warm, shimmering off the cobalt waters reflecting from a cloudless sky. Sitting on the edge of the small wooden dive boat, I began to pull on my wet suit. I was really going to give my lungs a run for their money now.

As I checked the pressure of my dive tank, I calmed my nerves by thinking about all the times I'd enjoyed scuba diving in various parts of the world, especially the Great Barrier Reef in Australia. Although, apprehension began to creep through the cracks of my confidence as I flashed upon the memory of that fateful time I'd hopped over from Australia to New Zealand to do some diving off the Poor Knights Islands. That particular day was clear and I was with a group of divers, taking pleasure in the ride out to the volcanic pinnacles. As is often the case, I was paired up with another solo traveler on the boat. George was a friendly, middle-aged American who had a number of dives logged in his book. We agreed to keep it a recreational dive and not go below one hundred feet, which would mean having to take longer decompression stops.

As we began our descent into the chilly water I began to gasp for air. I wasn't sure if I was having a panic attack or just feeling incredibly constricted by my full, hooded wet suit. My tank felt heavy and awkward; I wanted to rip it off my body. The dive master suggested I return to the boat and sit this one out. I floated on my back, breathing deeply, calming myself.

"No no, I'm okay," I assured him. I was surprised at myself. In well over a hundred dives, this had never happened to me before. I shook the feeling that maybe this was a bad omen, and once below I felt my usual underwater euphoria, blissful and meditative.

We pointed out various fish and slipped in and out of the caverns for which the area is famous. I looked at my gauge and noticed that we were rapidly going past our agreed descendent rate, and I tried to grab George's flipper. He ignored me and actually began swimming deeper into the black below. I tried to get a visual on him but couldn't. After finishing my safety decompression stops, I surfaced.

There was George facedown, floating in the water. The dive

master flipped his body over. George's face was pale and his vacant eyes looked skyward. Blood poured from his mouth and nose. One of the other divers tried to give him CPR, but it was too late. His gauge showed that he'd been 180 feet toward the ocean floor. Apparently he'd panicked, dropped his weight belt, and shot directly to the surface. His lungs had popped like paper bags.

With that image in my mind, I took a long look at the diving companion I was entrusting myself to, a boy sitting next to me, with glowing white teeth, young enough that he should still be in school. "Will my heart and lungs hold up to this next challenge?" I wondered. There was only one way to find out.

I pinched my nose and rolled backward into the clear azure blue Indian Ocean, making a slow descent. That first, potentially lethal ten feet squeezed and expanded my tender lungs. What the hell, they'd already made it to the top of Kilimanjaro! Feeling braver, I descended down to twenty. I was surrounded by multitudes of groupers, puffers, rainbow-colored parrot fish, yellow snappers, angel and butterfly fish, scorpion fish, goat fish, yellow trumpets, unicorn fish, giant wrasse, lobsters, and even a spotted stingray. My smile was so wide I could barely keep my regulator in my mouth. After two years of struggling to walk on land, it was so relaxing, almost embryonic, to float along weightlessly, surrounded by the reassuring tranquil sound of my own breathing.

Later, while making notes in my dive book, I noticed the date:

January 2, 2002. It was two years to the day since my accident, and I had spent it diving in the Indian Ocean.

Another milestone passed.

For the next part of my trip I continued on to South Africa to work on my book. During one stop, I stayed overnight with a family I'd met in the all-black township of Inanda, outside Durban, a place where Gandhi had lived for fourteen years. As I walked the main road the next morning, a police car came to a screeching halt in front of me. "Do you know where you are?" the white policeman asked incredulously. "Do you see that you're the only white person around? In my thirty years on the force you're the first I've seen walking around here alone—and a woman!" It was clear that he was furious that I would endanger myself like that.

The police officer insisted that I ride patrol with him. We came across two black policemen tending to a man who had just been shot dead, empty bullet casings strewn around his body. They too were astounded to see me there. After listening to two hours of carjackings and robberies streaming over the police radio, it was hard not to feel discouraged. The cop I was with admitted that he alone had shot twenty-five people during his career.

Continuing my drive down the Garden Route along the coast, I pulled over at the Bloukrantz Bridge, compelled by the sign that read "World's Highest Bungee Jump." Not only did I stop to photograph the jumpers, but I couldn't resist taking the 709-foot plunge myself. I questioned my decision as I was snapping back and forth, while dangling upside down from that elastic rope. I felt as if my eyes would detach from their retinas.

Next stop Uganda, to white-water raft the Zambezi River, in hair-raising class-five rapids. My river guide was missing his two front teeth from the same falls we plummeted down in a sheer rocky drop.

I watched as the raft in front of mine headed over the falls, its contents tumbling like apples being shaken from a tree. There was a collective scream as each person grasped for nearby branches in order to avoid being sucked into the surrounding swirling eddies. I realized in that moment that I was becoming too cavalier. In the past I had always loved the thrill of pushing the envelope, challenging myself to the utmost extreme, in order to taste my own mortality.

But as I shakily pulled my raft from the water, it occurred to me that I didn't need to do that anymore. I had already gone as close to the edge as one can go. I had determined that if I could do the things that my old adventurous self would do, then that would prove that I was still the person that I had once been. But I came to realize that throwing myself off bridges and waterfalls wasn't doing it. The old me no longer existed. I needed to respect my body. I had conquered the mountain; I had reached my goal. Wasn't that enough? Why, then, wasn't I satiated? Why was I still feeling so unsettled? Even the accomplishment of climbing Kilimanjaro began to feel like a means to an end. If not to get myself back to doing the things I used to do, then what had I come back for?

"Hi, sweetheart. I'm so proud of you making it to the top of Kilimanjaro!" My dad was thrilled when I called him from the Mombasa airport on the way to my next stop, Lamu Island back in Kenya. I appreciated his enthusiasm, knowing how hard it must have been for him to let me go again after coming so close to losing me. "I have a bottle of Sancerre chilled for you." He knew it was my favorite wine. "I can't wait to see your pictures when you get back. I love you."

Sadly, my father had been struggling with his own mortality as he continued his battle with bone cancer. He had defied the odds and soldiered on for five years since the initial terminal diagnosis. It was disheartening to see that during this time of extreme illness his religion seemed to give him little solace and inner peace. He asked me about some of my spiritual practices and how to meditate. Sometimes I felt that I had survived to help him with his journey, to reassure him that at the time of passing we really do reach a point of acceptance and that it was all right to eventually let go.

But for the moment I was brimming with news about my climb and my dive. "I love you too, Dad. I'll call you soon."

Friends invited me to stay with them in a beautiful house near the beach on Lamu Island, a short flight from Nairobi. Every day an eager young houseboy ran out to buy the catch of the day from the local fishermen and then cooked dinner for us. One morning, I had gone out windsurfing and had relished the sun on my face and the freedom of the breeze as I cut along the water. Then, as if out of nowhere, a chill wind suddenly brushed against my heart. I remember thinking that it would be the last time I would feel so happy for a long time. Unable to shake the dark feeling, I returned to the house, and when I couldn't get my cell phone to work or got an Internet connection I decided to catch a standby flight to Nairobi. My friends were incredulous. "But we're having fresh lobster for dinner," they said, trying to persuade me to stay.

I knew something was wrong. Sure enough, in the taxi in Nairobi, there were a number of messages on my cell phone from Andrew. I waited until I had safely returned to the house where I was staying before returning his call. "You're not going to believe this, but Dad just suddenly died." My father's heart simply stopped beating on February 14, 2002, Valentine's Day. I berated myself for being so far away, thinking of all the times I'd rushed to his bedside and he'd managed to pull through.

"Look, I live here and I couldn't even make it to the hospital in time to be with him," my brother said.

Here I was, alone in Africa, with news that brought me to my knees. I could barely make my way to the airport.

I wrote his eulogy while on the plane. Andrew picked me up at the Denver airport and we went directly to the funeral home.

When I pulled back the sheet, in his hands Dad was holding a photo of the three of us at the opening of one of my exhibitions in New York. I was flanked by the two men I had known the longest in my life, my brother and my father. They looked so handsome in their suits.

At his cremation, I made sure to watch his body, sporting his ever-present silk handkerchief in his breast pocket, being pushed into the flames. It was the only way my father's death seemed real to me. I realized that my own near-death experience helped me to get through that heartbreaking day. I knew this body was just a shell, that right now he was experiencing the same all-encompassing love and light I once had. It gave me great comfort knowing that. We left a *New York Times* crossword puzzle, with a pen, next to his urn. Everyone laid down a white rose. Back in Dad's apartment we found the bottle of Sancerre chilled in the fridge, just as he had promised. We drank a toast to him after the funeral.

A friend painted a lovely scenario for me: to imagine my dad as a sailing ship, with sails billowing and rigging glistening in the setting sun, heading from shore as I and all who love him wave good-bye. As he sails away and gets smaller and smaller and finally drops over the curve of the horizon, to imagine that there are other loved ones and family members on another distant shore who are gathered and waving to him in welcome anticipation. Visualizing him as that elegant boat gave me great comfort.

I believe when you lose someone who's loved you, that person's energy and spirit become a part of your being, and you become more powerful than you have ever been. I needed all the guardian angels I could get because mine were working overtime.

After my father's funeral I was scheduled for another surgery, this time to remove to the long scar racing up my abdomen from the ventral hernia operation. The original wound hadn't healed properly, and I wasn't able to move comfortably. I would need to be resutured and begin the recovery process over again.

On the day of my scheduled surgery, the galley for *Faces of Hope,* my photo book of children from around the world, arrived. I grabbed it and ran to my appointment at the hospital.

I didn't seem to be tolerating the anesthesia well, due to the number of surgeries I'd had, so I agreed to have the three hour abdominal and arm surgery while under a local anesthetic.

"You're so Zen," Dr. Johnson said as she pierced my stomach with the knife. Stuart, the sympathetic nurse, made feeble jokes as my sweaty hand gripped his. Two and a half years after the accident—and I was still having surgeries. I was getting used to having so many procedures that it hadn't even occurred to me to ask a friend to accompany me.

"We just keep sewing you up and throwing you back out there," Dr. Johnson laughed as she finished her suturing and tossed my snakelike curl of a scar into a kidney-shaped metal bowl. I lay back, drained from the physically and emotionally invasive surgery.

And then she did a remarkable thing. Dr. Johnson took time

out of her demanding schedule and sat down next to me on my hospital bed as I lay there in recovery. She opened my book with me and looked at every single picture. I was so touched.

"I can't believe it's taken me this long to finish this book," I said, closing it up.

"I can't believe you're actually here to finish this book," she responded with a smile, squeezing my hand.

CHAPTER 19

There is no end to the process of getting your life back— eventually, you have to come down from the mountain. And as any good mountain climber knows, the real success is surviving the descent.

It didn't take me long to realize that because the physical healing had demanded so much energy, my emotional repair work had taken a backseat. Insomnia was making my life intolerable. When I did sleep, I was still plagued by nightmares, tortured by violent dreams filled with lacerated bodies; screeching metal; and, for some reason, drowning. But worst of all is the recurring dream I still have in which I am waiting for the bus with friends. When it arrives I am so paralyzed with dread, I can't get on. Everyone leaves without me.

I once read that we have about sixty-six thousand thoughts a day and that two-thirds of them are fear based. We are taught to be afraid of what we can't control. Fear can be a good emotion for self-protection; if the danger is physical it leads us in one of two directions: fight or flight. But so often we create a narrative around it in our own minds, and it's getting caught up in this fabrication that paralyzes us.

Faith is the other side of the story—it's what enables us, despite our fears, to fully engage with the unknown. This trust in ourselves, the world around us, or a higher power, requires us to question and examine our lives and define our own inner truths; and it makes us willing to explore. Unlike beliefs, which are something we obtain from the outside and are ingrained in us via our traditions or heritage, faith is something that resides within us. It's what gives us the courage to move forward.

I knew that in order to chase those demons and come to terms with my own deep-seated fears I would have to face them straight on. I was eventually going to have to get back on that bus in Laos. I had to prove to myself that, unlike in my nightmares, I could do it. This time, I would be in control. I had to have faith.

Almost as soon as I made this decision, I was coincidentally sent to Thailand on a magazine assignment, kayaking in the southern islands of Tarutao. Afterward, I took advantage of being in the country to travel north to the Aek Udon International Hospital in Udon Thani to surprise Dr. Bunsom. It was January 2, 2003, exactly three years since I was last at the hospital. Being there brought up a tidal wave of intense emotions. I felt the air suck from my body, as if remembering what it was like not to be able to breathe. It was sobering to be in the familiar room where I had once lain so bloodied and broken and to relive that initial harrowing night. My feeling of sheer exhaustion, desperate to stay alert while holding on for medical help for so long, came back to me with full force. And even then, when I had finally arrived at a real hospital, I hadn't known if I would make it or not. But I had made it, and in great part because of the skills of this extraordinary doctor. I was delighted to find that Dr. Bunsom still worked there. I waited for him in the hallway, sitting next to a woman holding a live chicken. When he came by, he walked right past me, so I called out to him, telling him my name.

"You're so short," he exclaimed with a smile, seeing me standing up, and not bedridden, for the first time. "I had no idea you were so small," he teased as we hugged each other. With tears in my eyes, I thanked him for saving my life.

We visited for a while, and I got to show him pictures of my family. I told him about the new books I was working on, about windsurfing in Hawaii, scuba diving in Micronesia, snorkeling among beluga whales in the Arctic, and, of course, the Kilimanjaro climb—slices of my life that nearly never came to be. And then it was his turn to get teary. It was a very poignant morning as we stood in the intensive care unit, where I had once spent weeks, hovering between life and death.

He asked after my brother and Joe and Jerry. Eventually, the nurses came in and laughed, reminding me at how many phone calls I had received during my stay. "We were moved at how obviously people must care for you very deeply," the head nurse said.

Dr. Bunsom and I chatted about the differences between health care in the United States and Thailand. "I had never seen anyone with injuries of your extent, and I haven't since." He had worried about the adequacy of his hospital and his own limitations. He told me that he'd had to answer to a whole board of doctors to explain why he cut me open as he did. "But I knew something was wrong when we couldn't get a breathing tube down your throat. Luckily, we were able to revive you as we nearly lost you—you basically flatlined and very nearly bled to death right there on the operating table."

That explained the reaction I'd had after my abdominal surgery in San Francisco. I was so sure that I had died when I was on the operating table back at home, but it turned out that it must have actually been a response to this previous surgery. I was later told that if you are placed in the same mental state, sleep or hypnosis, or in my case being put back under anesthesia, then you could revert to that experience.

I told Dr. Bunsom how little spiritual or mental encouragement exists in the American medical system, and, as a contrast, I reminded him how he had arranged for my visit to the Thai temple.

It had been wonderful to see him again, but eventually he

had to get back to work. After we said our difficult good-byes, I went out into the street, and there was his last gift to me—once again, he had organized an ambulance to drive me wherever I wanted to go. This time, though, I would be sitting in the passenger seat.

I had other unfinished business. The next day, I continued up to Laos, determined to find Alan, the British aid worker who had played such an important role in saving my life, driving me the eight hours from Laos to Thailand in the back of his pickup truck. This time, I enjoyed the scenic drive over the Thai-Lao Friendship Bridge from Thailand to Laos.

Alan had no phone or fax and the last I'd heard he'd opened a business in Vientiane. I scoured the town to no avail. I eventually came to the conclusion that some angels were meant to find you—you weren't meant to find them. I had one last drink at a local bar before calling it a night, when the man next to me mentioned that he had lived in this city for six years.

"Really? Have you heard of Alan Guy?"

"Sure," he told me. "He lives in Kasi."

Bingo! I headed up there the very next morning.

Kasi, nothing more than a truck stop, is about forty-five minutes south of where my accident happened, and is the town where I had been brought to the small roadside clinic. The area was still very rural, and I was forced to hitch rides on the back of passing motorbikes, sometimes sandwiched between whole families. Just as I remembered, no one spoke English, and there were still no phones.

Eventually, a man approached me and indicated that his son would take me to Alan's house for fifty thousand kip, just over five dollars. His school-aged son looked mortified at being pimped like that, but I was desperate and set off in the darkness with him. Sure enough, I found Alan's name on the door of the house. Unfortunately, my elusive angel had just left town and was back in Vientiane—where I had just been! I left a warm note, along with a copy of the article I had written describing the event that had touched us both.

The next morning I returned to the clinic in Kasi, where I had initially been treated for my injuries. It was as awful as I re-membered, basically a ramshackle shed in a cow pasture. I was mortified to realize that the room where this young man had sewed up my shredded arm was actually a storage closet. I sat quietly in front of the door, lost in remembering my trauma and fear, reflecting on how truly amazing it was that I had been able to come out of a situation like that alive. The local staff hovered about, clearly upset by my distress and not un-derstanding why this foreigner was staring at their cow pasture so intently.

Unable to communicate with them in any other way, I brought out photos of my zipper-stitched arm. A young man with a flop of dark hair looked over my shoulder at the picture I was holding.

He suddenly became very animated, pointing at the blue closet door, and then across the pasture to the room where I had lain for so many hours.

He broke into a grin, which I immediately recognized. "Oh my God, you're the one who sewed up my arm!" I exclaimed. Much to his embarrassment, I embraced him. *"Khop chai lai lai!* Thank you so much for saving my life!" I said. He told me his name was Khamthat Chanthamoughhong.

He wasn't a doctor, or even a nurse, but a lab worker with no medical training. He'd just happened to be there that day. He showed me the hook and wire similar to the one he'd sewn my arm with—it resembled an upholstery needle, something one would use to sew up a sofa. Still, his resourcefulness managed to stop the bleeding long enough to save me.

A middle-aged gentleman with dyed black hair walked up to me with one word.

"Oxygen!"

He spoke no English at all, but all these years later he remembered the one word I kept repeating over and over.

"Who are you, were you there that night?" I asked him, slightly confused. A number of locals were now sitting around a table with my translator, and I was beginning to feel like Dorothy coming out of her tornado dream.

To my surprise he told me he was Dr. Seng. There had been a doctor there? And then it came back to me from the muddy depths of my memory. He had been called in later that night from the village, but the situation was beyond anything he had ever seen before. He apologized for being so helpless to do anything. I looked around and understood. This was no place to have surgery. There weren't even screens on the open windows.

"I hope that one day I can come back and bring you very large canister of oxygen," I told them. It was a six-hour trip just for them to get X-rays. Even photocopies of the patients' paperwork had to be done in Vientiane.

"And who are you?" I asked another man with a familiar-looking face. "I remember you at my bed. Are you a doctor too?"

"I'm the gardener," he told me. "I mow the grass and pick up the leaves." I was touched. Even he had been at the foot of my bed until late that night, his face racked with concern.

People began to stream out of the buildings in curiosity, gathering to look at the pictures of my damaged body. Many had been there that night, three years ago, and they expressed their concern at feeling so helpless in the situation. The women hugged me and wept. They were astounded to see me alive, even more so to see me walking. These good people were basking in the celebration of this miracle as much as I was. Our lives had become intertwined by this experience. I will never forget that I am here today because of the kindness of these strangers.

It was now time for the hardest journey, the one that fueled my nightmares. The bus to Luang Prabang pulled up—and, unlike in my dreams, I did get on. The villagers waved good-bye. I took one last look at the brave young man who had sewed up my arm, and the bus pulled away.

It had the same rickety wooden interior as the one I'd been on that terrible day, the same plastic chairs lined up down the middle. I remembered the sliding windows so well, with no safety glass. This time I chose the aisle, and way in the back. I watched the tourists reading their guidebooks, and as I took long deep breaths I was amazed by my own outward composure. As we passed the steep inclines I could only estimate where the collision had actually occurred on this remote jungle road.

There was no reason to feel fear anymore, I told myself; fear was just a thought. I had allowed it to liberate me, not victimize me. For now it was all in my mind, and there was no reason to be anxious.

And then suddenly—unbelievably—a huge bus whipped around a hairpin turn and hurtled straight for us. People screamed. Not again, I thought. The bus clipped us and was gone.

I gripped the seat in front of me. In that instant my mind had flashed back to the accident. How could I possibly have placed myself in this situation again?

"Oh my God, that was close," sputtered the girl next to me in a panic. In a second, fate can send a bus crashing into you and change your life—or not.

We pulled over at a rest stop, and everyone disembarked for something to eat. The smell of burnt meat sizzled in the warm air. I sat on some steps quietly taking in the scene around me. I listened as a tourist next to me complained about the food, the weather, the lack of things to do in Laos. Why wasn't she kayaking in Thailand? she lamented. Suddenly a craggy old Laotian woman with deep wrinkles and black-enameled teeth parted the crowd and made a beeline for me with a determined eye. Raising her hands over my head she invoked a mumbled prayer, and tied two thin white strings around each of my wrists. I recognized them as protection cords, blessed by holy people, and to be worn until they fall off. Asking for nothing, she then melted back into the crowd as quickly as she had appeared.

"What was that about?" the man sitting next to me asked. I smiled, for I felt I knew. I was being watched over. I told this small cluster of strangers about my last incredible bus ride on this very road. The girl who had been complaining looked at me.

"Wow," she said quietly. "I guess my vacation's not so bad after all."

By the time I disembarked in Luang Prabang, I felt I had truly come full circle. I immediately went to visit my friend Oliver, who hadn't seen me since New Year's Day of 2000. He had no idea I was coming and greeted me with a huge hug before running out to the temple across from his gallery to organize a resurrection ritual with the monks. These were the same saffron-robed monks I had been photographing the morning I left for the bus ride, a lifetime ago. We made food and monetary offerings to the monastery, a symbol of thanks to all the gracious people who helped save my life. And then we sat down to toast our reunion with a few cocktails that we dubbed "survival mojitos."

That night Alan sent me an e-mail with his mobile phone number. How do you thank someone for saving your life?

"It's the anniversary of your rebirth!" Alan greeted me when I called. But our celebratory conversation soon turned somber. He told me that his twenty-one-year-old son had been killed three months after my accident, on that very road—mowed down from behind by a drunk on a motorcycle—while on his way to a wedding. "His spine was broken and his skull crushed."

I couldn't believe it. That night I lay in bed thinking about Alan and his son. Why, I couldn't help but wonder again, not me?

In June 2003 I traveled to Holland to pay my first visit to Roel and Meia, the Dutch couple who had been in the accident with me. They had since gotten married and lived in a comfortable home with a lovely little garden. One of Roel's promises to me as I lay dying—and so thirsty—in that remote Laotian village was that one day, after we got out of there, we would all have a drink together. And there we sat, in the warm sun, drinking a bottle of wine. And now, a two-year-old tow-headed boy played at our feet.

"I had such a problem mentally adjusting to all that had happened to me," Meia admitted. We had discussed this in our e-mail correspondence, but I was not fully aware of how difficult the challenges of her physical disabilities had been. "I had trouble keeping my balance. I saw doctor after doctor. My life was filled with rehabilitation; I was sullen and angry," she said. "But the worst part was the emotional adjustment. It felt so big to me that I had survived something so traumatic that I wanted to alter my life. I changed my job to find more significant work. Roel and I got married. We had a baby. I wanted to find meaning in why I had survived." It was a question Meia and I had both taken on, and it inspired our continued communication with each other.

We had leaned on each other during the stormy days of our recovery, and I knew how Meia had struggled with this question. I, on the other hand, had not sought change but felt a confirmation—that more than ever I wanted to continue on the path that I had been on, photographing the world around me. I still felt passionately that it's what I was destined to do. I cared about people in need and wanted to continue doing stories that drew attention to their plight. Meia and I had both been tested and it brought greater clarity to both of our lives.

It seemed natural that when one comes so close to death one wants to create life. I didn't have the same compulsion. Until I felt I could get as excited about having children as I did about an assignment in Afghanistan, it seemed wisest not to go that route. Love, I had come to realize, does not always take the form of a single partner or child; it lies in everything, every moment surrounding us.

"I feel that life and its emotions are so fluid," I had written to

Meia at one point. "Maybe life's purpose is not to strive to obtain constant happiness, but to find fulfillment in our lives, in whatever way is meaningful to each of us."

As the woman he had just proposed to lay injured in that hospital, Roel too had gone through his own soul-searching. He had kept a meticulous diary, and he shared some poignant passages with us that detailed his own fears of losing someone he cared so deeply for. He also filled us in on some of the memories that we had filed far away for the sake of our own self-preservation. It became an evening filled with love, tears, and gratitude as we celebrated the fact that we had gone through the ring of fire and come out on the other side. In the last letter that I received from Roel and Meia, they announced that they had just had another baby boy.

CHAPTER 20

As I moved through the world, reconnecting with the people whose lives I'd touched and had affected me, I knew I'd come back for a reason. But I was still working on what that reason was.

In the summer of 2003, I was invited by Richard Gere's organization, Healing the Divide, to photograph the Dalai Lama at some of their sponsored events, including his speech to a crowd that jammed and overflowed Central Park in New York City. One evening a number of my Tibetan photographs were presented in a slideshow at Avery Fisher Hall as the Dalai Lama was speaking. The opening photo was one I had taken of him in Dharamsala, as we walked along the lovely bamboo-shaded lane from his home to his office. Passing one of his ever-present protective Indian guards, suddenly the Dalai Lama stopped. Placing one hand on the soldier's, which was holding a rifle, he chanted a prayer and moved on. It was a lovely symbolic gesture of peace. The guard simply beamed. After a few moments of this image alone on the screen, the Dalai Lama himself walked out onstage. The crowd cheered.

His Holiness was also giving a week of teachings at the Beacon Theatre, which was packed with familiar faces, from movie stars to laypeople, all part of the Buddhist community. Every morning the stage would fill with Tibetan monks wearing banana-shaped yellow hats, and their soulful harmonic chants resounded through the auditorium.

The Dalai Lama sat on a throne and wore a baseball cap to shield his eyes from the spotlights. One day he was deep in the middle of reading from his teachings when he was so overcome by the words of his prayers that he spontaneously burst into tears. Many of us were taken aback, having never seen him cry before, and it brought most of the audience to tears as well. It was a moving lesson in compassion, this sympathy for the suffering of others.

This really hit home when Tashi, a Tibetan monk and a dear friend from Nepal, saw me in the lobby and expressed his shock. "You're whole!" he exclaimed, touching my arm in disbelief. "For weeks we sat meditating; I imagined you as broken body parts. It was deeply troubling. I visualized putting your pieces back together."

"Well, it worked," I told him with a hug.

His delight was obvious.

I was pleased to see Richard and his lovely wife, Carey, again. They invited me back to their place to have dinner with their family. I adored Carey's down-to-earth parents, Jim and Suzanne, who I'd taken on a trip to Tibet and stayed friends with ever since.

It felt a little surreal as Richard and I sat in the apartment with our feet up, watching a baseball game on television, drinking white wine, and discussing the Dalai Lama's teachings. Richard is one of the most erudite students of Buddhism I have ever met, and certainly one of the most devoted. I could barely keep my head above water in the esoteric discussion, and, frankly, I was finding the baseball game just as perplexing.

Richard knew I'd undergone a number of surgeries since I'd last seen him, and at one point he asked me how I was doing. "Much stronger. I've been healing really well," I told him. I admitted that at first I was pretty self-conscious about the scars, but the criticisms didn't bother me as much anymore. "If people don't like my appearance, they can look at something else." It was summer in New York, and I was wearing short sleeves.

He laughed, and turning from the game, put his hand on my damaged arm.

"You look just fine," he told me, peering over his glasses. It was a very reassuring and welcome comment, coming from the sexiest man in the world. Compassion, it's a powerful thing.

Leaving Richard's apartment and walking down the buzzing streets of New York I thought about how meaningful it had been for me to be back in touch with so many of these like-minded friends for the last two weeks. I had been feeling isolated in my personal struggle of healing for so long and this spiritual community helped me recognize the yearning to continue the next steps of my inward journey.

As I reflected on these teachings of the Dalai Lama, I thought of another influential teacher who had given me strength and peace, Thich Nhat Hanh, the Vietnamese monk and Nobel Peace Prize nominee who has lived in exile from his own homeland since the 1960s because of his writings protesting the war.

In June 1999, six months before my accident, I visited the Plum Village in France to photograph and attend a retreat with Thich Nhat Hanh, or Thay, as he is respectfully called. My schedule included a five o'clock wake up and a full day of walking, working, and meditation. In Plum Village, as in his monastery, which I had visited in Vietnam, there is an emphasis on working together as a community, and this retreat center was a little more lenient than others I had attended. For a start, we were allowed three meals a day rather than the customary two. Talking was sometimes allowed, although whenever a bell, phone, or a clock would chime, it was a signal for all activity and conversation to cease. The pause brought you back to the moment at hand for deeper awareness and immersion. Even now, in my busy world, the ring of a phone causes me to stop and breathe, a reminder to come back to the present.

On my second day there, Thich Nhat Hanh was scheduled to give a talk. As I arrived, he was already sitting onstage in front of a small gathering of people. At seventy-three years his face was still unlined and his calm presence radiated.

"There are only one hundred ninety-one days left to the new millennium," he said through a translator. "Remember to make each one count. Breathe, smile, relax." He discussed the importance of ancestors: how "we are constantly reborn in others." I thought of the Dalai Lama's explanation of rebirth: that it is like a candle flame, lighting first one then another. It's not the same candle, but the same origin.

Thich Nhat Hanh spoke about right livelihood, choosing to work in a job that would help others and not harm them. He encouraged us to find a spiritual *sangha,* or community, in which to keep up the practice during our busy, stressful, productive lives.

"Sometimes we do very much, but not for the sake of peace. Sometimes we do not do anything, but we are for peace. So instead of saying, 'Don't just sit there, do something, we can say the opposite: don't just do something, sit there.'"

Afterward, when I was photographing Thay, he told me that I should write a book or an article about the practice of meditation. "Books are your legacy."

He explained that with air, water, and even love, we are different from one moment to the next. To have children or produce a book is output. You are giving something of yourself to be absorbed by others. You don't have to die to be reborn. You can offer yourself to others through your insight, and your care. You can offer your heart. "And in that way you will live on and be remembered," he told me.

"And isn't that basically what we all want," I thought, "whether it's through someone reading our book or a partner in a relationship, someone to bear witness to our lives?"

That is what, I suppose, my intentions were when I first wrote about the accident. The chronicle of my story and subsequent healing had initially gone out as an e-mail to my friends. I was touched by their concern and, besides wanting to communicate with those who cared about me, I found it cathartic to write about it. My message soon began circling the Internet. I was somewhat astonished that anyone was interested in my little tale of personal struggle, and even more so when *Outside* magazine wanted me to write an article for them on the subject. I was equally grateful when the editor, Hal Espen, requested a follow-up piece about my Kilimanjaro climb two years later.

The letters and e-mails sent by strangers moved me to the core and gave me a great source of strength to continue on with my goals. Many people wished me well in my restoration. Others had suffered from such awful injuries, either to themselves or to loved ones, and they wrote to me of their own ambitions and aspirations to heal. A flight attendant wrote and told me she had found my article in a magazine in an airplane seat pocket. Her friend was in a coma, struggling for her life, trying to recover from brain damage after a car accident from a tire blowout in Egypt.

As much as I felt honored to receive such messages, it also made me a little anxious to read about so many near-death experiences. I was trying to regain confidence in the world around me, and sometimes it was difficult to be reminded of how much potential disaster is out there. The correspondence often left me feeling "There but for the grace of God, go I," and was a reminder that I was not only lucky to be alive but to have managed to regain so much of my physical strength

While some were emotionally difficult to read, there were many others that inspired me to keep up my longing for adventure. A young woman wrote and told me how my story had encouraged her, despite a twisted ankle, to get to the top of Kilimanjaro with her four friends. She had thought of me while standing on the roof of Africa.

The letters sent to me from well-wishers over the years inspired me as much as I did them. They were part of the sangha that helped to heal my spirit. It took some time for my mind to catch up with my physical progression. The nightmares eventually subsided, and I was now healing beyond all expectations.

Even Susan Hobbel, my physical therapist, attested to that on my last appointment with her. She had given me a hug when she heard about my Kilimanjaro climb. "Your recovery from a trauma of this magnitude was incredible," she said. "Your progress from lying eviscerated in a third world country to taking a kayaking trip in Alaska and then climbing to the top of Kilimanjaro is one of the most amazing recoveries I've ever been involved with."

235

I was so appreciative of all the work she had done with me. Susan told me that meeting someone who had started on crutches, who couldn't walk, then go through all the surgeries I did, was one of the biggest successes of her career. "That a person can be so terribly injured and set back so far and then respond to such a level of performance is a great example of what you can achieve if you're motivated. I think it's why people like me become physical therapists. It makes me really appreciate what the human body can do. I'm so proud of you." And then she told me to get on my way. We could meet for coffee, but I didn't need to see her professionally anymore.

By climbing Mount Kilimanjaro I had proved to myself and others that I was able to make a physical comeback, but I yearned for a more spiritual reason for being. I realized that if I were able, in the e-mails we shared, to encourage people to follow their ambitions, then it was time to fulfill my own: to realize my dream of circumambulating Mount Kailash. I hoped that the sacred pilgrimage I had so longed for would yield some answers to the higher questions that I was still seeking to answer.

CHAPTER 2 1

And so to Mount Kailash. In the early summer of 2004 I flew to Nepal. I was delighted to once again see the mud-brick homes and green rice fields of the Kathmandu Valley appear through my airplane window. This little landlocked country still felt like home to me, although many of my expat friends had, because of the political turmoil, now relocated to other parts of the world.

It was there, in the sticky monsoon heat, that I met my traveling companions for the trip, Nancy and Dennis. Nancy was a nurse in her early fifties. We were surprised to discover that we were practically neighbors, living two streets away from each other in San Francisco. Dennis was an artist from Canada in his midsixties. With sandy hair and a ruddy face, he seemed a good-natured outdoorsman. Both were concerned about their age and expressed a little apprehension about the physical challenges the altitude and hike would present. After my Kilimanjaro climb I wasn't feeling overly concerned for myself.

Still, it was not going to be an easy trip since no trains, buses, or planes travel anywhere near Mount Kailash in the western region of Tibet. The three of us planned to take a bus to the Tibetan border and then transfer to a four-wheel drive. A local outfitter supplied us with tents and a couple of Nepali Sherpa guides, Tendi and Kailas, as well as Wangchuck, our impressive cook. This being a politically sensitive area we also had to have a mandatory Chinese guide. He introduced himself as Sunny, but with his beak nose, long black trench coat, and dark sunglasses we nicknamed him Roy Orbison. His incessant chatter was peppered with condescending remarks about the Tibetans.

"Look how cheerful they are. You never see an unhappy Tibetan," he said as we passed ragged Tibetan road workers chipping away at the rocks with crude-looking tools.

"They don't look too thrilled to me," I said. It looked like they were digging their way through the cliffside with a teaspoon. Roadwork has been an ongoing business since the Chinese moved into Tibet, and new roads were cropping up everywhere— everywhere, that is, except on the way to Kailash. We were told that was about to change, as roadways and even a new airport were being planned for the remote western area. It was difficult to imagine the immediacy of air travel in such inhospitable terrain and thin air. An important aspect of the pilgrimage to Mount Kailash by devotees was the journey of getting there. With each bump of the rocky surface we tried to convince ourselves that we were in fact earning more merit.

Our four-wheel drive rumbled on through the lush emerald green jungle past thunderous waterfalls, as we followed the Kali Gandaki River. Forests and their wildlife have been obliterated here at an astonishing rate. In previous years I had hiked down the mountainside at least a half-dozen times due to road closure and landslides caused by Chinese logging and the lack of trees to hold the mud loosened by the monsoon rains.

Eventually our vehicle pulled into the small town to Nyalam. Long-haired Tibetan men were playing pool on outdoor tables that lined the streets of every town. With Chinese receiving work and monetery incentives to reluctantly move to the remote regions of Tibet, the result is massive unemployment among Tibetans. Han Chinese currently outnumber the six million ethnic Tibetans in their own country. With the Dalai Lama gone from his homeland, there was no holding back the Chinese influence.

Our guide had neglected to make reservations, and there was now no room at the Snowland Guest House. The manager directed us to a brand-new Chinese hotel across the street—what appeared to be a soulless box with beds. Typically, there's usually a price list for every item in the room, from the television to teacups, which makes one wonder what goes on in these places. As we were preparing to check in, Dennis took a photo outside the hotel. Suddenly, as if waiting their entire lives for this very moment, an onslaught of green uniformed guards immediately rushed out of the building waving their arms in protest and squawked at us angrily. Apparently, photographing hotels wasn't allowed. We ended up camping outside that night, an icy wind buffeting the walls as we huddled in our tents.

The next day we packed ourselves back into the four-wheel drive. The landscape was as dry as the moon. At times it felt as if we were driving through a car wash of sand. Dust devils danced and twirled across the plains. Particles seeped into our noses, clothes, and camera gear, which started to make unwelcoming gritty sounds with each turn of the lens.

It didn't take us long to realize that our driver had brought only one cassette to listen to for the duration of the three-week drive. We soon knew it by heart and sang raucously along with the Tibetan rock band. Even soft-spoken Dennis shocked us at one point with the resounding cry of, "Is everybody all right out there?" until we realized he was just mimicking the lead singer.

As we looked out the window at the arid land, we saw the occasional yak-hair nomad tent. Women were milking yaks and children herding goats along the roadside, snapping at their behinds with small twigs.

"Life must be so unbelievably different for them now in India," Dennis said.

And he was right. Through India's generosity, the Tibetans were allowed to settle there in temporary refugee camps. Here, they were encouraged by the Dalai Lama that the great job ahead of them now was to preserve their religion and culture.

The change in climate was a challenge for the refugees coming from the cool mountains of Tibet and settling in the heated plains of the Himalayan foothills. While many died working on the roads, even more were overcome by tuberculosis and malaria. (While photographing in one of these camps in central India I too had contracted a bad case of the disease.)

The first six hundred refugees were eventually given some land to settle on in South India. They had only hand tools, axes and knives, to cut through the brush. Wild animals were a big problem. Elephants, tigers, bears, and wild boar roamed the jungles, and the refugees had to surround the camp with kerosene lamps and light firecrackers to scare them away.

They faced even more problems once they managed to clear the land. In Tibet many had been nomads, roaming with their cattle and selling butter and milk. They knew nothing about farming. In the beginning, a couple of technical advisers from India supplied tractors, seeds, and fertilizers, but for three years they still couldn't get it right. Planting was a complete mystery to them. They couldn't understand why nothing would flourish, not realizing that you have to plant row by row and use only ten pounds of seed per acre, not one hundred. When they finally did get something to grow they ended up picking all the corn and leaving the weeds—they didn't even know the difference between the two. Eventually, a Swiss specialist came to teach them and the settlement now cultivates about eighteen hundred acres a year. Looking out the window at this barren land we could see what a challenge it must have been for them to learn how to grow and tend crops.

Still, in a relatively short period of time the refugees have managed for the most part to create a self-sufficient life for themselves. In Nepal, where the land is scarce and often unproductive, the Tibetans have opened trekking shops and restaurants in the cities of Kathmandu and Pokhara. With the initial help of foreign aid, traditional carpet weaving has slowly evolved from a small-scale craft into an industry that has become not only the backbone of the refugees' livelihood in Nepal but also the largest earner of foreign currency in the country besides tourism.

In an interview with me at his home in Dharamsala, the Dalai Lama noted how the Chinese have helped to keep the Tibetan culture alive. As we discussed the future of his country he told me that if the Chinese had treated the Tibetans well, looking after them while considering them equals, and had a properly planned program of progress in Tibet, then after thirty years the situation may have been different. But because the Chinese have done so many negative things to the entire population of Tibet, inside and out, the Tibetan people have lost their faith in them. They have no hope. "I'm sure the Chinese had no intention of helping the Tibetans to become more unified, but they have certainly contributed," he said. "To love your family is easy, but to love your enemy is really an expression of compassion."

CHAPTER 22

I tried to keep this considerate philosophy in mind when Sunny threw our schedule off by insisting that Saka Dawa, commemorating Buddha's birthday, was in fact a day earlier than we had been told. Our goal was to arrive at the base camp of Mount Kailash in time for this full-moon celebration, but Sunny told us we had been misinformed.

"How can five thousand people be wrong?" I asked our guide. Still, he insisted we forge ahead, and we missed our day to acclimatize to the rarefied air. As a result, outside of Saga, a remote town in western Tibet, at 11,500 feet, I developed an intense bout of altitude sickness and, with a severe headache, vomited for two straight days and nights. Although I'd been to similar heights before, it was the first time I'd been this weakened by altitude illness. I was so depleted I wondered whether I should abandon the trip.

Tendi and Kailas took turns checking on me at night. I sipped Coca-Cola when I should probably have been on an IV drip, but it was enough to keep me going. It was torture to get back into the car and drive for twelve-hour days while feeling so nauseated. Finally, after an grueling week crammed in the Land Rover, we spotted the shimmering blue water of Lake Manasarovar with the snowcapped peak of Mount Kailash in the distance. It looked like an oasis in this vast desert, and we could barely believe what we were seeing.

Kailash is where South Asia's great rivers are born: the Indus; the Sutlej; the Tsangpo, which becomes the Brahmaputra; and the Karnali, which merges with the Ganges. At its foot lies the most venerated of Tibet's lakes, Manasarovar, revered by both Buddhists and Hindus. At nearly fifteen thousand feet above sea level, it is the highest freshwater lake in the world.

We jumped out of the car to add our own string of colorful Tibetan prayer flags to the accumulated frayed pile and admire the lake's pure iridescence. Sunlight danced on the small windswept whitecaps. Despite the chilliness of the water, a long-haired Indian sadhu, or holy man, was fully immersed, cleansing his sins by washing himself and drinking the water.

We opted, instead, for the nearby hot springs. It was our first real wash in ten days.

Tents and people dotted the valleys in throngs as we pulled closer to the mountain. We had been right about the date after all. We started pitching our tents by a gurgling river that wound down from the mountain.

"Now that we're camping a day early, there will be an extra charge for the grass-cleaning fee," Sunny lifted my tent flap to inform me.

"Because we're a day early? I practically died from altitude sickness due to your negligence! And what the hell is a grass-cleaning fee anyway?"

Sitting outside of our tents, the three of us agreed that there was no way Sunny/Roy Orbison could accompany us. Sensing our reticence, Sunny declared that there was a problem getting enough yaks to carry all the gear.

"Well, you'll have to stay behind then," Dennis said. Sunny looked relieved at this suggestion; he had managed to save face, and we had managed to get rid of him.

We later found out that he'd never even been here before.

I set up my tent facing the giant snow cone of Mount Kailash. It was hard to imagine that I was actually there. This 22,028-foot-high mountain, considered by most Buddhists to be the center of the universe, has never been scaled; to do so would be considered sacrilegious. A single kora, or circumambulation, is thought to wash away a lifetime of sins, and Buddhists believe that making 108 circuits secures nirvana in this lifetime. I would be satisfied to get around once, but, even so, doing this on Saka Dawa, Buddha's birthday, would give us a slight edge in our hopeful journeys to enlightenment.

Nearby, the deep resounding call of a conch shell filled the air, announcing the arrival of an eminent Tibetan lama, Angton Dorje, who resided in a nearby monastery. Monks trailed after him, blaring long horns and clanging resounding cymbals as he circled through the crowd performing an elaborate ritual blessing of the area. Dennis, Nancy, and I followed the entourage into the lama's tent to hear his chanting prayers and watch as he lit butter lamps. We each received a blessed protection string from him to tie around our necks.

We were greeted by a festive atmosphere when we emerged from the tent. A large circle of people had formed around a lofty wooden pole draped in colorful prayer flags representing the elements. Everyone cheered as two large trucks helped pull it up for the ritualistic annual raising, the flags now madly flapping in the wind, their invisible prayers blowing steadily toward the impressive snow-covered mountain before us. We were each passed a handful of *tsampa,* roasted barley flour, and with a mighty "om" the crowd threw them in the air as an offering to the gods. We, like the rest of the pilgrims, had now been properly blessed. It was time to begin our journey around the mighty Kailash.

At the start of the four-day thirty-three-mile trek, my altitude sickness had fully subsided, and I was feeling quite fit, but now Nancy and Dennis wondered if they were strong enough to make it. Though we'd managed to lose Sunny, we were still accompanied by our devoted Nepali crew: Tendi, Kailas, and Wangchuck.

In addition, we hired a couple of local Tibetan yak herders who loaded our gear and provisions onto the backs of their pack animals.

The first day, my stamina was good and I walked ahead of Dennis and Nancy, pausing for them along the way. We were entertained by some of the small tests of devotion we encountered. In one, if you were successfully able to squeeze your body through a tunnel formed by boulders, it signified that you were free of sins.

"Isn't that a little unfair for heavy people and foreigners?" I asked Wangchuck, our paper-thin Nepali cook who slithered through every crevice like soap on a rope. I imagined my Western hips wedged halfway through the hole, like Pooh hankering after the honey pot.

The Tibetan word *kora* means "to circle around a sacred place." For Tibetans, this pilgrimage refers to the passage from ignorance to enlightenment, from self-centeredness and materialistic obsession to a deeper sense of the relativity and connection of all living beings. This concept of rising above the material realm was exemplified, as we continued on, by what looked like a graveyard of discarded bits of clothing and nonessential body parts. Rocks were piled into cairns and adorned with abandoned New York Yankees hats and T-shirts, amid piles of hair, fingernails, and the odd tooth. This shedding of possessions symbolized relinquishing the past, readying oneself for the new life that would come after crossing the pass. I left a lock of my hair. (I believe it's where I also left my bandanna, though I have to admit it wasn't intentional.)

Day two was the toughest. We climbed the 18,700-foot Dolma La in a heavy snowstorm. Pilgrims slowed to help one another as we painstakingly placed one foot in front of the next, gulping in the thin air. One young man stopped to offer me a plastic bag to wrap up my camera and protect it from the fierce elements. Such a communal determination was the only way we'd make it over the pass—we all wanted to see one another succeed.

At the top we were greeted with the smell of crushed juniper incense. Crowds of people had gathered for a bite to eat and to sip a hot drink, although thanks to the altitude I didn't have much of an appetite. Our Hindu Nepali guides loved our beef jerky, thinking it was yak meat, and we didn't dare dampen their enthusiasm by telling them otherwise.

I joined the laypeople, monks, and nuns in paying homage for having made it this far. It's common in the Himalayas to affix prayer flags at the peak of high passes to show respect to the mountain. Observing my own rite of passage I chose to add a string of white prayer flags to the others that were already snapping in the icy breeze. The white cloth symbolized air or wind, the breath of life, and each was imprinted with prayers and the image *lung ta,* a winged flying wind horse, suggesting that the prayers will race to heaven, sending forth blessings to all sentient beings.

Combating the cold and fatigue, I continued with my small ritual. Someone had created a makeshift altar designated to leave photos of loved ones who had not been lucky enough to make the trip to Kailash. I left the rocks that each of my young nieces had painted just for the occasion and, leaning their photos beside them, lit sticks of incense. I included a photo of Andrew with his arms around each of the three girls: Claire, Hannah, and Erin. Despite being far from home when each girl was born—Nepal for Claire, Sikkim for Hannah, Jordan for Erin—in each case I'd had an innate sense that they'd arrived in the world.

I made a simple wish as I laid the photos down. I hoped that when they were old enough they too would expand their world by traveling to other lands, to be influenced by this magical planet and the people who touch their lives, and to do so with love in their hearts and awareness in their souls—appreciating everyone they meet for each is a teacher in some way.

Wangchuk stood next to me on the top of the Dolma pass holding his own small ceremony for our shattered thermos, tying a silk scarf around its base and solemnly chanting a small prayer over it. I returned his grin when he looked up at me. "Yes, even Wangchuk is a little bodhisattva in his own right," I thought.

As I walked around the mountain, I knew it was important to continue visualizing those I cared about, as it's believed that even these thoughts bring good fortune to your loved ones. Walking with this intention made me think of the last time I had visited the Dalai Lama.

When I had visited his modest but modern home nestled in the forest overlooking the Kangra Valley, he greeted me warmly.

"Ah, you again," he exclaimed, taking my hand and holding it as we walked through his garden. He stopped to feed his pet parakeets, housed in spacious cages on his front lawn. "These birds," he sighed with exasperation. "We initially brought them here because they were injured. Now that they're better I keep trying to set them free, but they keep coming back to me."

"Maybe they're people you know who've come back as birds," I teased. "Everyone wants to be near the Dalai Lama. They probably missed you." We both laughed.

I apologized for taking time away from his incredibly busy schedule. I wanted him to know that it was with good reason that I had arranged our meeting, that I genuinely wanted to help him and his people. When I assured him that I have the best of intentions, he turned toward me suddenly, as if reading my eyes. Nobody has ever looked at me so deeply.

"Yes, I know. And good intent is very important. Most important in all that you do. Never forget. Whatever your actions, it's the intention you hold in your heart that truly matters." We are human and we make mistakes. But his words have become an adage to live by, they have made me gentler toward others and myself.

Admittedly, kindness was a difficult emotion to tap into when we discovered that evening that our camp's oxygen tanks had been stolen—especially when we found that one of our hired yak herders was apparently the culprit and was charging us a "fee" for finding them. Poor Tendi had to hike back all those miles to fetch the tanks from where they had been hidden behind some rocks. He was familiar with the drill. When he returned he told us, "They stole our mattresses last time. And before that the toilet seat." I couldn't imagine what a nomadic yak herder would do with a toilet seat.

After hearing how risky this trek was and that people had died, Nancy, Dennis, and I were livid. We made it clear to the porter that this had better be the last time he held our oxygen hostage. He earned the nickname "bad-man yak-man" after that. And from then on we watched our gear more carefully.

The next morning we awoke to a dusting of snow as we packed up our tents. That day, as I walked, I felt the power of Kailash pulling me along. Unlike Kilimanjaro, where I had been concentrating on a grueling uphill climb, this was a heart-opening journey around the mountain. The kora felt laborious yet empowering.

We encountered many robust souls who were taking two or three weeks, or even months, to complete the circuit, making full body prostrations one after another for the entire distance. These devout practitioners joined their hands above their head, touched them to their throats and hearts, and slid facedown on the ground amid the rubble and snow. Many of them wore leather aprons and wooden mitts for protection, while others wore only bedroom slippers on their hands. Most of them were working on their 108 circumambulations around the mountain to ensure enlightenment. I couldn't even fathom that level of commitment and faith.

Prostrations are a popular form of worship in Tibetan Buddhism, a way to integrate mind and body through devotion. Chaku, an elderly Tibetan friend of mine, spent his days prostrating himself around the ancient stupa at Swayambunath in Kathmandu. One day he described what it meant to him.

"My nickname, Chaku, means prostrating," he told me. "A name I earned through my devotion to twenty-eight years of prostrations."

He sported a huge blister on his forehead to prove it.

"One day I realized that I should stop my work as a farmer and follow a religious path. Now I circumambulate the stupa all day long, from four o'clock in the morning until ten, and then again from three to six P.M.

"While I prostrate I meditate on various deities. I don't count the number of times I touch the ground, as it would disturb my concentration. If people stop and stare at me, as they often do, I incorporate them into my meditation. The women become goddesses, the men become gods."

That idea brought a smile to my face as I watched the pilgrims passing us.

That night I sat in the dining tent alone as Wangchuck served me a welcome steaming-hot dinner of *dal bhat,* rice and lentils. Dennis and Nancy were too exhausted to join me. I was also tired because I wasn't sleeping well, and not just from the cold and high altitude. My bones still hadn't seamlessly knit back together, and

it was uncomfortable to sleep on such a hard surface. Photographing in the cold was a challenge. The icy air split my fingers, which
were now open and bleeding. After dinner I went to visit Nancy,
to see if she could apply her nursing skills.

Her tent always amazed me. I stopped to admire the large ripe
white moon on the way, and a waft of incense and oils greeted
me even before I got there. "It smells like an Arabian boudoir in
here," I laughed, setting down a cup of tea for her. Her bedding
was always meticulously and comfortably arranged, and every
night she had a fragrant floral footbath before dinner. Nancy
bandaged my hands, and I reluctantly headed back to my own
tent, which was scattered with photo equipment, rolls of film, and
journals, and which for some reason always smelled of yak urine.

It was difficult to get up and face the early morning chill,
although my body always felt better once I started moving and
warmed up. During my day's walk I thought of everyone who had
been instrumental in getting me off that jungle road in Laos and
to a hospital. Despite my chest feeling pinched from the altitude,
my heart opened to the friends and family who had been with
me every step of the way. As I circled the base of that towering
snow-covered mountain I felt a force growing within me, a power
I never would have found without the challenges of the previous
four years.

This kora symbolized my personal odyssey discovering the
physical and spiritual strength I didn't know I had. Despite all my
worldly travels, the hardest journey turned out to be within myself.

I looked up that evening to see that yes, the stars did follow me, even here. Every night, there appeared to be more white in the sky than black. Every constellation shined, the Milky Way sweeping across the heavens like a sheet of pulsating diamonds. These were the same stars I had seen from the back of the pickup truck in Laos, the same sky that had held me before. I felt comforted by its consistency and said a prayer of gratitude.

And then I fell asleep in my snug sleeping bag.

Snow once again blanketed the landscape when we awoke the next morning. It was the last day of our expedition. Wrapped in my warm Patagonia fleece, I was regularly passed by Tibetan pilgrims dressed only in thin ragged clothing. They had no tents and carried their few precious belongings themselves. Despite the obvious discomfort of the elements, many were singing and most had smiles. I was encouraged by their determination.

I thought of others I had met on my life path who had stood up to their own struggles of hardship. When I first met Aung San Suu Kyi, the Nobel Peace Prize winner, she had been under house arrest for six years in Rangoon. The Burmese military refused to recognize her democratic win in 1990, instead seizing all power and holding her prisoner in her own home. I was inspired by her inner strength and determination during her ongoing struggle for democracy in imposed isolation.

This admiration prompted me to stop at her home during my first visit to Burma in 1996, but I was told that an interview would be impossible. It was by sheer luck that two days later I happened to be in Rangoon when she was temporarily released. Her secretary called to ask if I would like to come over and celebrate the New Year holiday with their family.

It was a fabulous day. The front lawn was teaming with National League for Democracy party members, dousing one another with hoses and buckets of water, as is the custom during the three-day water festival during the Burmese New Year.

I was granted my interview and ushered into an enclosed room, where I waited in the stifling heat. The room was devoid of furniture because Aung San Suu Kyi had sold it off piece by piece rather than be supported by her captors. For years she hadn't even had electricity. She emerged looking fresh, without a bead of perspiration on her brow, fresh jasmine flowers in her hair, wearing a lavender-colored sarong. She had the sniffles and even her purple hanky was color coordinated.

Aung San Suu Kyi shook my hand and seated herself regally, with absolutely ramrod-straight posture. Her youthful appearance and diminutive stature belied her fifty-one years. Despite her size, her presence was immense and seemed to encompass the whole room. I later observed that she managed the same self-composure even when among a huge crowd.

With a perfect English accent, she answered my questions articulately and at great length. We warmed to each other as we discovered that we had both lived for years in Nepal, worked extensively with the Tibetan culture, and traveled to Bhutan. With great intelligence and insight the dignified Aung San Suu Kyi was serious about her demands and desires as she related her significant messages to the world, but I noticed that her sense of humor and ability to laugh was never far behind.

Obviously missing was her immediate family: her husband, Michael Aris, who has since passed away from cancer, and her two children, Kim and Alex. The government continues to deny her family visas, and if she decides to leave Burma to visit them, she will not be allowed back into her own country.

"You've really given up a large portion of your personal life for your politics. Is it difficult? I wonder, do you ever feel alone?" I asked her at one point.

"No, I worry about my sons of course, as is only natural, but I do not feel alone because there are so many of us in the struggle together," she told me. "I think it is difficult to feel isolated in a situation like this, the very fact that we are subjected to so much injustice and persecution; it gives us a great sense of solidarity."

I was curious about how she got through her long periods of seclusion and asked her how she managed.

"Many factors have contributed to my inner strength, such as my Buddhist faith," she told me. "Also, my father was a major influence on me. As are my colleagues surrounding me who are so unafraid. But many people have stood up to adversity and come out stronger for it in the end. Certainly I was exposed to many attacks, but many others are just as dedicated and have had to put up with much physical hardship. It depends how far you are prepared to go."

Shortly after I left Burma, her secretary was arrested and Aung San Suu Kyi was placed back under house arrest. Eleven years later she still remains a prisoner in her own home. She is someone who continues to impress me with her indomitable spirit.

Slowly I put one foot in front of the other. I thought of the power of our minds and of Chunden, another monk I had met in Nepal, who told me his incredible story of devotion while being held for years in a Chinese prison.

"I was in Sera Monastery at the time the Chinese stormed it. They made everyone leave even though there were no guns there. They were determined to destroy whatever they could. They burned and tore our religious textbooks to shreds, crushed the statues, tore thangkas down from the walls, stripped all the blankets and bedding. I was later to learn that they used the religious scriptures for toilet paper and crushed the prayer stones to be used for roads to walk on. I was ill the night they came in, sleeping in a small side room and remained hidden there for a month, living only on boiled water. I was very afraid.

"A month later they found me. All the monks, lamas, *geyshes* [teachers] and *tulkus* [reincarnated lamas] were separated and spread out to different places. We were asked many questions during these *thamzing,* or struggle sessions. What do you believe? Why do you pray to these mud figures? Why do you read these texts? Most kept silent and refused to demean the scriptures or to talk at all. Many were shot, often while yelling, 'Long live His Holiness the Dalai Lama!'—and always it happened in front of a crowd.

"When I was caught I was made to work in the fields with many of the other monks. We were no longer allowed to wear our monk's robes and clothed in black shirts and pants. My head would spin from such hard work and lack of food. After seven years of this I applied to go the hospital in Lhasa, where I managed to stay hidden in a friend's house. For thirteen years I stayed in bed and never left this room. When the Chinese discovered me I claimed to be too ill to move. Every day they had someone to check up on me, fearing that I was making some sort of connection with the American army. I acted like I was deaf and had a lung ailment. In reality my body was very weak with worry.

"Actually, being a monk, I was happy to have this time because I just recited my prayers. Secretly of course, as I wasn't allowed any religious texts, but all the same I have a very sharp mind with many of the scriptures memorized so I used all my time of imprisonment for meditation. The Chinese have managed to destroy Tibet only superficially; they haven't managed to destroy our faith."

Many of the Tibetans I interviewed had been jailed for years yet could still muster forgiveness for their captors. Their inner strength when faced with the loss of everything they have ever known has been a great source of inspiration for me.

Instead of being beaten down by thirteen years of imprisonment, Chunden looked at it as an opportunity to practice his prayers and express his devotion. Like Aung San Suu Kyi, he had made a potentially debilitating incident into one of immeasurable positive circumstance. His situation had changed, but not his way of thinking. We had each learned that when confronted with hardships, we may not be able to be in command of what happens to us in our lives, but we can control our responses to it.

I continued on my trek, and, yes, it was demanding, but I felt light. I could now see that the divine power surrounding us doesn't necessarily respond directly to our burning questions and prayers but presents us with opportunities to discover our own answers. It wasn't the long-awaited Kailash trip that brought me what I had been seeking, but rather the clarity and awareness I had developed in order to make the trip. I saw that I wasn't meant to be here until now. It wouldn't have had the same meaning without all I had gone through to get to this point. I had finally found my peace.

"We make our lives so complicated," I thought as I walked. "Really, we are the same the world over. We all just want to have some work with a sense of purpose, safety, and health for ourselves, family, and friends, and most of all to feel love and be loved."

I felt humbled as I rounded the final turn in my hike around the mountain. Snow-covered peaks surrounded me as the wide expanse of open valley lay below and remnants of prayer flags fluttered over the river. Nancy was waiting up ahead. I stopped and felt the sun warm my face, savoring the moment.

I filled my lungs with the piercing cold air. My success, I now saw, hadn't just been in getting up a mountain. The problem with climbing one mountain is that there's always another on the horizon. My ongoing journey was a pilgrimage, full of peaks and valleys, with challenges, achievements, and lessons to be learned along the way. That logging truck in Laos had set me back, and defied me to find my core. But it had taken finding a stillness within myself to realize the answer to my question of why I had survived: for this breath. To be truly aware of each precious moment of time, right here, right now. For this very moment is all we have.

Each day as I had trekked around the mountain, visualizing all the people I cared about, I could feel my heart expanding, embracing all the beings knit together with me in the web of life. Over and over, I remembered my revelation at the moment I thought I was dying: nothing is more important than this seamless interconnectedness. The commitment the Tibetans around me brought to their devotions suddenly had a new resonance. I found myself grinning at the next group that straggled past me. We were all in this together, all companions in the pilgrimage of life.

AFTERWORD

Although this has undoubtedly been the worst experience that's ever happened to me, in a way, the accident in Laos has been the greatest. Once you've been hit by a logging truck, nothing else really seems so bad. It's truly a gift to be given the opportunity to overcome adversity and come out a stronger person for it.

The challenges I have endured have brought a renewed empathy to my work. I continue to photograph the lives and situations of people around the world, in pursuit of the universal human connection. This has led me to document endangered cultures and cover social issues such as children's rights, refugees, the tsunami in Sri Lanka, the aftermath of Hurricane Katrina, poverty in America, and women's issues in Afghanistan, Africa, and Asia. The pain I have faced has helped me relate to the hardships of others. I realize now it's not about chasing the story. It's about being part of the story.

Having viewed my mortality from a front-row seat has given me even more incentive to follow my heart and live my life to its fullest. Now each day seems like a gift, one giant postscript. When you get right down to it, the fear of death is nothing compared to the fear of having not lived a life to its greatest extent, with authenticity, awareness, and gratitude.

When I arrived in Sri Lanka, in January 2005, eight days had passed since the tsunami had hit. I found a car and a driver named George who, I believe, thought we would be taking a leisurely tour of the tea fields. After a week of my encouraging him to continue on along more than sixteen hundred miles of the worst-possible, most potholed roads, dodging wild elephants, Tamil Tiger insurgents, and a continuous array of soldiers brandishing AK-47s, he calmly inquired, "Madam, should I be buying clothes?"

The devastation we found rocked us both. The initial shock of the tragedy seemed to be wearing off and the enormity of what had happened to people's homes, their lives, their loved ones seemed to be sinking in. Relief was rolling in from all over the world, yet in many places the aid was still unorganized and often unavailable. Although millions of dollars had been donated, what these people needed most immediately were a few rupees to help them get by. I took to folding small amounts of money into squares and discreetly passing them on with the shake of a hand as we parted ways.

I stopped to photograph a man sitting in a chair amid a pile of rubble. Instantly, he called out, "Have a seat!" There he was, offering me the one thing left standing in his home! As if that wasn't enough, he shimmied up a tree to get me a coconut, and we stood, on a slab of concrete, drinking coconut milk in what was once his kitchen. Another man brought me tea. A woman gave me shells, the only possessions the ocean had left in her home since sucking away everything else.

I accompanied a young woman who was revisiting the remains of her house for the first time. It was where her two-year-old daughter had been ripped from her arms. The mother's face lit up with the memory as she picked up a teddy bear, a child's dress, a baby bottle. Then she lost herself to tears. Next door, a man was chinking through the debris with a small knife, looking for remnants of his life—an identity card, a bankbook, a rupee note.

Of the eight thousand residents of one small town I visited in Batticaloa, five thousand died. That's 60 percent of its population. Saris and clothing were left embedded in the barbed wire, set up to protect against wild animals, where many of the bodies had been trapped in its grip. A few odds and ends were scattered: cooking pots, photographs with cracked glass, clocks stopped when the wave hit at 9:22, Buddhist statues that mysteriously remained standing. But mostly there was just ruins.

On the beach, human bones had started to wash up. A woman who appeared to be in shock walked alongside me. As I turned to ask if she was all right, she began madly gesticulating toward the sea, indicating that it had taken her two children. Beside herself with anguish, she attempted to throw herself into the ocean. I pulled her back and held her as she wept. Inconsolable, she buried her face in the sand.

No matter where you are in the world, a mother's anguish is universal. Many felt the profound guilt of being unable to hold on to their children. Men who managed to grab on to palm trees live with the image of seeing their families swept away before them.

It was the end of the day, a milky dusk. I stopped to photograph an elderly Muslim man, his arms lifted to the heavens while clutching a small prayer book. He chanted prayers over the five freshly dug sand mounds before him, the graves adorned with small white flags flapping in the salty wind. Tears openly flowed down his cheeks as he raised his face to confront the sea that had killed his family. Our eyes met and his were so overwhelmed by grief that I was compelled to take his hand. The heartache became a shared, palpable connection as he told me it was his wife and four other family members he was burying, their bodies only just found after two weeks. We stood like that for some time, the unlikeliest of connected people, bound by the rawest of human emotions. There was nothing I could say. As I moved to turn away, I heard his soft voice call out just above a whisper, "Please," he implored, "don't forget about us."

And so the pilgrimage continues. One breath at a time.

ACKNOWLEDGMENTS

An invisible red thread connects those who are destined
to meet regardless of time, place, or circumstance. The
thread may stretch or tangle but it will never break.

—CHINESE PROVERB

My red thread stretches far and wide. Although some of the names of the people in this book have been changed, I am especially grateful for all those I met during my journey of survival. I wouldn't even be here to write this book if it hadn't been for the kindness and resourcefulness of strangers. These people have now become intrinsically intertwined in my life.

I want to thank the extraordinary relay team of people who were so instrumental in saving my life in those first twenty-four hours after my accident. Roel and Meia Snelder, Anne Thomas, and the others whose names I don't even know, who deviated from their travel plans to come to my aid. A resounding *khop chai*

265

acknowledgments

lai lai to all the caring people at the Kasi clinic in Laos, including Khamthat Chanthamougkhong, who initially sewed up my arm. A special heartfelt thanks to my personal angels, Alan Guy, the British aid worker, and his wife, Van, who drove me all those hours in the back of their truck to get me to Thailand (Alan, please call me. I still owe you a beer); and Michael Bakalar and Joseph DeMaria from the Embassy of the United States in Vientiane, who risked their lives to meet me and open the Thai-Lao Friendship Bridge in the middle of the night so that I could continue on to Thailand for medical treatment.

Much love and thanks to the commendable doctors and nurses at Aek Udon International Hospital in Udon Thani, Thailand, especially Dr. Bunsom Santithamnont and Ms. Tuk; and to my friends Oliver Bandmann, Joe Cummings, Jerry Alexander, Morris and Lyn Dye who immediately rallied together to keep the communication lines open and to arrange help so quickly. Much appreciation to the array of doctors and health-care providers stateside, especially Dr. Preston Wong, Susan Hobbel, Dr. Jann Johnson, Dr. Paul Cianci, Cathy Hammond, Dr. Daisy Sundstrom, Byron Russel, Dr. Helen Jackson, Dr. Christopher Zachary, and Dr. Lana Sandahl.

The greatest gift of all was to come back to feel the love from friends and family, especially my brother, Andrew, his wife, Beth, and his much-adored daughters, Claire, Hannah, and Erin, who have given me the immense strength and inspiration to be here right now. Thanks to my supportive parents, Frank and Sonia

Wright, who prodded my wanderlust then gave me the wings to fly, albeit sometimes a little too close to the sun.

A raised glass to my outstanding, loyal tribe of friends, too many to name, who saw me through the long haul of my healing, each aiding me in their own special ways during my recovery: Carmine Giordano and Hideo Yoshida (hands down the best cooks in San Francisco), Bob Condon, Jacqueline Butler, Tom Shadyac, Dana Harrison, Carol Bolduc, Christi Phillips, Elliot Marseille, Jeff Greenwald, Lisa Gosselin, Jen Leo, Lauren Cuthbert, John Flinn, Lynn Ferrin, Julie Evans, Richard Gere, Suzanne and Jim Lowell, Olga Murray, Danielle Machotka, Nancy Newton, the Osborne family, and Bob Thurman, who supplied me with healing talismans.

Much appreciation for the ongoing support from friends and colleagues at Geographic Expeditions, the National Geographic Society, and the Discovery Channel.

The events in this book are based on the best of my recollections. Some conversations have been condensed and streamlined to evoke the scene with more clarity.

I am indebted to those who have given me a platform to tell my story. To David Friend, David Schonauer, as well as the editors at *Outside* magazine who originally commissioned and helped edit the two-part article: Hal Espen, Stephanie Pearson, Brad Weiners, Amy Linn. Also to Todd Jones and the editors at *Yoga Journal* who felt the story worthy enough to run as a completely different version in their magazine. A heartfelt wish of loving kindness to

acknowledgments

all those who felt moved to respond to those articles. I wish you safe travels on life's sometimes tumultuous path.

Thank you to Stuart Krichevsky, my assiduous literary agent, a being worthy of enlightenment, who fortunately for me remains in the human realm. With enduring encouragement and unwavering faith he continued to believe that this accident-prone photographer could actually write a book. Hats off to his hardworking staff, especially Kathryne Wick and Shana Cohen.

From there a huge debt of gratitude extends to those at Hudson Street Press who were instrumental in publishing the book: Luke Dempsey who helped edit and shape my sensitive manuscript, Ted Gachot for his superb copyediting, Anna Sternoff for all her help and support, Elizabeth Keenan and Marie Coolman, and to Lucy Kim for her gracious collaboration and beautiful execution of the cover. Thanks to my dear friends Tim Cahill, with a raised glass to his partner Linnea, who, sadly, in one of life's ironic twists was tragically killed in an untimely car accident while returning from a day of skydiving, Linda Watanabe McFerrin, Janis Cooke Newman, Christi Phillips, and Lynn Ferrin for their sage editing advice and inspiration as the book progressed. Special thanks to Larry Habegger and the editors I've worked with in the Travelers' Tales series. Heartfelt appreciation to His Holiness the Dalai Lama for supplying such a noble foreword and years of spiritual guidance, with much special thanks to his secretary and staff.

I was bobbing along the frozen waters of Antarctica, when I got

acknowledgments

the call that Penguin was interested in acquiring my manuscript. As I looked outside my ship window, watching icebergs nearly the size of small countries float by, I realized that I was, ironically, completely surrounded by penguins. Somehow it seemed like an omen. Signs—they're all around us. You just have to keep your eyes and heart open.

—Alison Wright

San Francisco

PHOTO INSERT CREDITS

Top of the Dolma-La Pass . . . Alison Wright, 2004

I have been going to Tibet . . . Steve McCurry, 2005

The Dalai Lama . . . Alison Wright, 1998

Dodging bullets . . . Unknown, 1990

Three years after my accident . . . Alison Wright, 2003

Khamthat Chanthamougkhong . . . Alison Wright, 2007

My arm, in between dressings . . . Andrew Wright, 2000

Roel and Meia Snelder . . . Alison Wright, 2000

With my brother, Andrew . . . Ms. Tuk, 2000

Dr. Bunsom Santithamnont . . . Ms. Tuk, 2003

On a return visit to Kasi Clinic . . . Alison Wright, 2007

Happier times. With my nieces . . . Andrew Wright, 2006

Me on top of Mount Kilimanjaro . . . Arusha, 2001

The Dalai Lama greeting me . . . Unknown

tenacity + resiliency p5

68 69 74 259 260